A HISTORY
OF
THE CHURCH IN WALES
IN THE TWENTIETH CENTURY

The Most Reverend George Noakes,
Archbishop of Wales

A HISTORY
OF
THE CHURCH IN WALES
IN THE TWENTIETH CENTURY

by

The Revd. D. T. W. Price

Senior Lecturer in History
St. David's University College
Lampeter

1990

ISBN 0 85326 026 5

Contents

Illustrations

vii

Foreword

by the Archbishop of Wales

This is the first full-scale study of the Church in Wales in the twentieth century. The story is a fascinating one, taking us from the end of the bitter struggle over disestablishment, through the period of retrenchment and reconstruction to our present time in which the Church in Wales, although now recognized as playing a significant role in our nation's life, has to proclaim the Christian Gospel to a society which has become very largely indifferent to its message.

We can be grateful to the Revd. William Price for a carefully researched and well-balanced work which not only throws light on the recent past of our Church, but also provides pointers and possibilities for its future development. Despite the problems which confront us, the overwhelming feeling which emerges from this survey is one of hope. How can it be otherwise if the Church continues to remain true to the Gospel on which it is founded.

✝ George Cambrensis

The Purpose of this Book

For some time I have been increasingly aware that many people, including many members of the Church in Wales, are not very well informed about the history and organization of the Church.

One can think of many matters on which some, perhaps many, members of the Church in Wales seem to be a little unclear. When, how, and why did the Church in Wales acquire its twentieth-century independence? Did the Church in Wales want to be disestablished? What is the Church in Wales's relationship with the Church in England and with other Anglican or Episcopalian Churches in the world? Does the Archbishop of Canterbury have any authority in Wales? What is the position of the Queen with regard to the Church in Wales? How is the Church in Wales organized today? Why are the services of the Church in Wales different from those of the Church of England? What is the ecclesiastical position of an individual who moves from living in England to living in Wales, or vice versa? These are some of the questions which I have been asked over the years.

This short work is intended to provide an outline of the history of the Church in Wales in the twentieth century, an account which must include some discussion of how and why disestablishment occurred. An Appendix indicates briefly how the Church in Wales is organized today, at provincial, diocesan, and parochial level.

It is hoped that this book will be of use to members of the Church in Wales, to interested observers in other churches in Wales, and to visitors, Anglican and non-Anglican, to the Church in Wales.

My credentials for venturing to write this book are that I was baptized into the Church in Wales in my infancy (the son of a Church in Wales priest, but the grandson of a Welsh Calvinistic Methodist, or Presbyterian, minister), and then after spending most of my younger life in England I returned to Wales in 1970 to teach History, including Welsh History and Church History, at St. David's University College, Lampeter.

More recently it has been a source of great joy to me to serve as non-stipendiary Priest-in-Charge of the small country parish of Betws Bledrws, near Lampeter, and I have had my parishioners and their questions about the Church in Wales very much in mind as I have been writing this account.

I have also visited every Anglican church building in Wales, and so I can claim a more than theoretical knowledge of what the Church in Wales is like at 'the grass roots'.

Material for this book has been collected from many periodicals (including *Yr Haul, The Welsh Churchman,* and *Highlights*), from Governing Body papers, and from many other books and articles on the Church in Wales. Some of the more helpful are listed at the end of this book. At an early stage in my reading it became clear to me that a very large book could be written on the History of the Church in Wales since 1920, and my main problem in presenting this short account has been to select themes which seem to me to be important. Much else could have been discussed. Other authors would probably have chosen other topics. I am deeply grateful to Archbishop George Noakes and to Bishop Eryl Thomas and Mrs. Thomas for reading the typescript and for making many perceptive comments. All errors are, of course, my responsibility.

The Church in Wales was disestablished on 31 March 1920, and the publication of this work on 31 March 1990 will thus mark the seventieth anniversary of the modern Church in Wales as an autonomous and self-governing Church within the Anglican Communion. Few of the members of the Church in Wales now can remember the battle for disestablishment. To most of us it is an event from long, long ago.

The Church in Wales has done more than come of age; it has reached three score years and ten. It seems to me that, although it took a great deal of time and mental readjustment, the Church in Wales has now much more self-confidence in its essential work of bringing the Gospel of Jesus Christ to the people of Wales. It is now much more visible in the life of Wales, which is today less seen as 'the land of chapels' than once it was. If *Under Milk Wood* were being written today there might well be a parish church and a vicar in Llaregyb!

Lampeter

William Price

1

A Brief Account of
the Disestablishment Campaign

(i) Why?

No one knows when Christianity reached Wales, but it seems likely that there were Christians among the Roman soldiers during the Roman occupation of Wales. The centuries after the departure of the Romans were important as the 'Age of Saints' in Wales, when David, Deiniol, Dyfrig, Illtud, Kentigern, Teilo, and a host of others established a firm basis for Christianity in Wales.

By the end of the twelfth century Wales had been organized into territorial dioceses, under the primacy of the Archbishop of Canterbury. From then until 1920 the four Welsh dioceses of Bangor, Llandaff, St. Asaph, and St. Davids were integral parts of the Province of Canterbury, just like Rochester and Lincoln. They underwent the break with Rome in the Reformation of the sixteenth century, at the same time as the Acts of Union between Wales and England were passed. Later, bishops and other scholars provided Welsh versions of *The Book of Common Prayer* and the New Testament in 1567, and of the Bible in 1588. The Welsh dioceses experienced the turbulence of religious change in the seventeenth century, when for a time the Church of England ceased to be the established church.

At the beginning of the eighteenth century the people of Wales were overwhelmingly members of the Church of England, with perhaps 5 per cent being Protestant dissenters (Baptists, Congregationalists, Presbyterians, and Quakers), many of them living in English-speaking areas along the border, and a tiny fraction being Roman Catholics, almost all of them in Flintshire and Monmouthshire.

The eighteenth century witnessed an amazing revival of religious practice, and the growth of Nonconformity continued apace in the nineteenth century. The Anglican Church lacked the machinery to adapt to new social and demographic conditions; Nonconformity was much more flexible. During the first half of the nineteenth century a Nonconformist chapel was opened every eight days in Wales. It was this dramatic growth of Nonconformity in Wales—much greater than that in England—which was to lead to the disestablishment of the Church of England in Wales.

The new dissent of the eighteenth century was Welsh Calvinistic Methodism. It began within the Church of England, but gradually it developed into a distinct denomination, with the formal split coming in 1811. For thirty further years the still growing body of Methodists remained closer to the Church of England than to the Protestant dissenters, who were also increasing in numbers, but by the 1840s the Methodists, partly because of the Oxford Movement, had thrown their lot in with the older dissenting churches. The religious census of 1851 revealed that almost 80 per cent of worshippers in Wales attended Nonconformist chapels, with fewer than 20 per cent attending the liturgy of the Church of England in Wales. A most significant result of the religious census was the disclosure that half the population did not worship at all. By 1882 the Nonconformists had 4,361 places of worship, 1,934 ministers, 2,469 lay preachers, 391,406 members, and 463,468 scholars in Sunday Schools, out of, be it noted, a total population of about 1,500,000. New chapels transformed the landscape, and especially the townscape, of Wales.

At a time of considerable Welsh cultural nationalism it was wholly understandable that many people should begin to question whether the church of a small minority ought to be the Established Church in Wales, its clergy entitled to received tithe from Nonconformist parishioners, who had also to pay their own ministers and to maintain their places of worship. Here was a rallying point which could unite the majority of Welsh people. The most distinguished historian of modern Wales, Professor K. O. Morgan, has rightly commented that during the second half of the nineteenth century Welsh society was led by Nonconformists, who focused all their social, economic, political, and nationalist grievances on disestablishing 'the alien church', the spiritual face of 'landlordism'. Disestablishment was not simply a 'religious' issue. Although there were distinguished Welshmen serving in the ministry of the Church, there was some truth in the commonly held perception that the Established Church was much more English in outlook than were most of the Nonconformist denominations.

The growth of the Liberal Party and the widening of the franchise encouraged the movement. By 1887 Mr. Gladstone, himself a high-church Anglican, was coming to favour the disestablishment of the Welsh Church, to please Liberal Members of Parliament in Wales, and after 1891 the Liberal Party was formally committed to disestablishment.

(ii) How?

Disestablishment required an Act of Parliament. The first parliamentary motion came in 1870, after the disestablishment of the Anglican Church of Ireland, but it was to be 50 years before the Anglican Church in Wales followed its Hibernian sister church. The Conservative Party supported establishment, so only during Liberal governments could supporters of disestablishment hope for success, although not all English Liberal Members of Parliament approved of disestablishment. Bills in the 1890s came to nothing for various reasons, and the issue was not raised again until after the Liberal victory of January 1906, when conflicts over church schools had aroused feelings against the Church. The religious revival of 1904-5 had also sharpened enmity between Church and Chapel.

But the government had many other problems to tackle, and the next Disestablishment Bill did not go through the House of Commons until 1912, following the deliberations of a Royal Commission on Religion in Wales and Monmouthshire between 1906 and 1910. A Bill of 1909 was withdrawn. Until 1911 the opponents of disestablishment could count on the Conservative majority in the House of Lords to defeat any legislation, unless the Liberal government were to take the drastic step of securing the creation of sufficient Liberal peers to gain a majority in the Upper House. The Parliament Act of 1911, however, reduced the powers of the House of Lords. Henceforth their Lordships could only delay legislation passed by the Commons.

In spite of great popular protests by members of the Welsh Church, of which the largest was in 1912 when a rally in Hyde Park and a meeting in the Albert Hall were attended in all by 15,000 Welsh Churchpeople and 5,000 from the Church of England, the House of Commons passed a Bill to disestablish the

Church of England in Wales for the third time in 1914. The House of Lords had lost its veto, and the Act received the Royal Assent on 18 September 1914, by which time leaders and public alike had more pressing concerns than the Church in Wales. It was eventually agreed that disestablishment should not take place for twelve months or until the end of the War, although the process of disendowment could begin at once. The Welsh Church Commissioners were nominated, and they began to prepare to deal with the pecuniary aspects of disendowment. No clergyman appointed to an office in the Church would thereafter be eligible to receive compensation for financial loss when the Welsh Church Act came into effect.

The religious scene in Wales had, of course, changed considerably between 1870 and 1914. All bishops appointed after 1870 were Welsh speakers—of varying degrees of competence—and this removed an old grievance of the Church being led by foreign prelates. The Anglican Church had increased its membership and it had greatly improved its organization and efficiency. New parishes had been created and new churches had been built, for example, 24 in the parish of Ystradyfodwg in the Rhondda between 1869 and 1904. In Llandaff Diocese between 1883 and 1905, the episcopate of Bishop Richard Lewis, 80 new churches and mission rooms were built, and 14 other churches enlarged. Many church schools were built, especially in the Diocese of St. Asaph. In the parish of Colwyn Bay £44,448 was spent on church building and extension between 1891 and 1911, and during the same years £97,385 was spent on schools, churches, and church work in the parish of Wrexham. Easter Communicants in St. Asaph Diocese increased from 14,214 in 1890 to 31,069 in 1912, while the Diocese of St. Davids had the highest number of Easter Communicants in proportion to its total population, 8.68 per cent, of any diocese in Wales and England. The average for the whole of Wales and England was 6.28 per cent. If the Church were disestablished in the Diocese of St. Davids, perhaps the Church of England ought also to be disestablished!

On the other hand Nonconformity had begun to lose its dominant place in the life of Wales, and the membership of the largest Nonconformist denominations had begun to decline. The Church fought long and hard to maintain its position, but in the end it could not withstand the House of Commons, even when a petition bearing the names of 103,224 Nonconformists in Wales who opposed disestablishment—the 'moderate Nonconformists' whom Bishop Owen of St. Davids sought to win over—was presented to Parliament. These Nonconformists opposed the appropriation of spiritual funds to secular uses, for the endowments of the Church in Wales were not be given to other denominations. Everyone, or almost everyone, was exhausted after the long and barren struggle, but the Church had greatly strengthened itself in the process.

The Act of 1914 dissolved every cathedral and ecclesiastical corporation in Wales, removed the Welsh bishops from the House of Lords, abolished the coercive force of the Church's courts, and diverted tithes from the Church in Wales to the local authorities. No longer would the Monarch appoint bishops and private patrons incumbents. Burial grounds which were not private gifts and which were still in use were to be handed over to the control of local authorities. (Many local authorities refused to accept the churchyards, and in 1946 they were vested in the Representative Body.) While all ecclesiastical law was dissolved as part of the law of the land, the ecclesiastical law of the Church of England was to 'be binding on the members . . . of the Church in Wales as if they had mutually agreed to be so bound'. All endowments given to the Church before 1662 were taken from it.

The delay in implementing the Act gave the Church the opportunity to reduce the financial loss of disestablishment. An Amending Act of 1919, passed by a House of Commons with a Conservative majority, preserved some endowments to the Church, and the Treasury made a grant of £1 million to the Welsh Church Commissioners, charged with transferring the Church's endowments to the local authorities, so that the Commissioners could pay commutation capital to the Representative Body. It was, in a sense, re-endowment to enable the Church to survive financially. The value of money and of tithe had so changed since 1914 that some alteration in the financial provisions of the Act of that year was essential. It was calculated that the Church had lost £48,000 a year of its income. Eventually, in 1942 and 1947, £3½ million was transferred, most of it to the County and County Borough Councils and the remainder, just under £1 million, to the University of Wales.

On 31 March 1920, the Wednesday in Holy Week, the Church in Wales became a disestablished church. No longer was there an established and privileged church in Wales. All denominations were legally equal in status. The Church in Wales ceased to be part of the Province of Canterbury, although it remained in full communion with the Church of England. King George V was still the 'most gracious Sovereign Lord' of the people of Wales, but he was no longer Governor of the Church in Wales—but he retained, by virtue of being Monarch, his stall as First Cursal Canon of St. David's Cathedral, the royal canon of a cathedral within a Church to the disestablishment of which he had given his Royal Assent! The leaders and members of the Church in Wales had not sought this freedom, and they were deeply apprehensive about the future. The Welsh Church Act had, in the words of the future Bishop G. C. Joyce, been intended 'to smash the machinery and rob the safe'. How would the Church survive?

(iii) Border Parishes etc.

The border between Wales and England did not everywhere coincide with diocesan boundaries. A number of parishes which lay partly in Wales and partly in England and some parishes of recent creation, which while wholly in Wales had once been within ancient parishes in both countries, were, if their inhabitants so wished, permitted to remain, and still do remain, within the Church of England. These parish churches or daughter churches are, roughly from north to south, Saltney Ferry, Higher Kinnerton, Whitewell, and Rhydycroesau in Clwyd, Middletown, Leighton, Trelystan, Snead, Churchstoke, Hyssington, Sarn, Kinnerton, Old Radnor, Discoed, Presteigne, and Michaelchurch on Arrow in Powys, and Llangua, Dixton, and Wyesham in Gwent. On the other hand the parishioners of Llansilin, which is mainly in Clwyd but which extends into Shropshire, voted to stay within the Church in Wales. Thus the ecclesiastical Province of Wales is not coterminous with the Principality. Parts of Wales are not in the Church in Wales, but it does contain a small portion of Shropshire, the township of Sychtyn in Llansilin parish, presumably the only place in England in which the Anglican Church is disestablished.

Those ancient parishes within English dioceses but geographically entirely in Wales, together with more recent parishes formed out of ancient parishes wholly in Wales, had to join the Church in Wales. Thus, Penley left Lichfield for

St. Asaph, Criggion, Forden, and Montgomery left Hereford for St. Asaph, and Evancoed, Knighton, New Radnor, and Norton left Hereford for St. Davids.

Parishes wholly in England also had no option. They were transferred to the Church of England. The Church in Wales lost fifteen parishes in and around Oswestry—Hengoed, Kinnerley, Knockin with Maesbrook, Llanyblodwel, Llanymynech, Melverley, Morton, Oswestry St. Oswald, Oswestry Holy Trinity, St. Martin's, Selattyn, Trefonen, Welsh Frankton, Weston Rhyn, and Whittington. The severance of the important, and very Welsh, town of Oswestry from the Diocese of St. Asaph was a bitter blow, presumably brought home to the Bishop of St. Asaph every time he passed through it, as he was almost inevitably obliged to do, to visit the Archdeaconry of Montgomery within his jurisdiction.

Dewi Sant, the Welsh church in Oswestry, remained in use until the 1970s, its services unintelligible to its diocesan Bishop of Lichfield. It was not the only Welsh church in England in 1920, although it was the only one which had been previously in a Welsh diocese. Half a dozen served the Welsh diaspora in London, three fulfilled a similar need in Liverpool, and there were also Welsh churches in Birkenhead, Chester, and Manchester. By 1990 there are two Welsh churches in London (St. Benet's, Paul's Wharf, in the City and Dewi Sant, Paddington), and one in Birkenhead, and regular Welsh services are, I believe, held in an Anglican church in Liverpool. These churches in England were, and are, outside the Church in Wales, coming under the authority of the local English bishop. The formerly Welsh-speaking church at Chubut in Patagonia has always been under the jurisdiction of the Anglican Bishop in Argentina, between 1946 and 1962 a Welsh-speaking native of Lampeter!

2

The Church between 1914 and 1920

(i) The Government of the Church

The Act disestablishing the Church had been passed in 1914, but the decision to suspend its operation until the end of the War allowed the Church's leaders breathing space to plan for the future. In the event they were also to have 16 months after the cessation of hostilities to prepare for undesired independence. A few leaders, including the Bishop of Bangor, at first felt that the Church ought to do nothing to anticipate disestablishment. Let there be chaos! There was always the hope that a Conservative government might come into power and repeal the Act. But the majority of the Church's leaders, led by the Bishops of St. Asaph and St. Davids, felt that such a policy of doing nothing would be far too risky. 'Be prepared' was their watchword as they pondered on the parable of the wise and foolish virgins.

A meeting at Shrewsbury on 11 December 1914 set in train the future organization of the Church. A Joint Committee was appointed 'with full powers to take such steps in matters of business as they consider necessary under the Welsh Church Act' and also to discuss the question of forming a Representative Body. This was needed because on the day on which the Welsh Church Act came into force all the property of the Church in Wales, the cathedrals and churches (except for the church plate and the furnishings of churches), the bishops' palaces, deaneries, vicarages and rectories, churchyards, glebe land, and endowments, ancient and modern, would be vested in the Welsh Church Commissioners. Not until a Representative Body had been created could the buildings and the modern endowments be returned to the Church. Ancient endowments and tithe were to be divided, as we have seen, between the University of Wales and the County Councils.

The Joint Committee spent two and a half years preparing proposals for consideration by the four Diocesan Conferences. Since the total membership of the Diocesan Conferences was 3,000, it was decided that a Convention, made up of 100 representatives of each Diocesan Conference (one bishop, 33 clergymen, and 66 lay persons), should be held to consider the plans. The Joint Committee had prepared schemes on the Governing Body, the Representative Body, Diocesan and Ruridecanal Conferences, Vestry Meetings, Parochial Councils, Patronage, and the Election of Bishops, but the Convention, which met in Cardiff in October 1917 for four days, discussed only the setting up of the Governing Body and the Representative Body. The other matters would be left to the Governing Body when it met.

The Cardiff Convention, much influenced in its deliberations by Mr. Justice Sankey, later Lord Chancellor, resolved that there should be an elected Governing Body, containing bishops, clerical representatives and lay representatives. This would be the legislative authority in the Church, charged during the period before disestablishment with 'making constitutions and regulations for the general management and good government of the Church and the property and affairs thereof', while a smaller elected Representative Body would hold in trust the property of the Church. The functions of the Representative Body were 'to hold all property of the Bishops, Clergy, and Laity of the Church in Wales and for others, the special trusts pursuant to the provisions of the Welsh Church Act, 1914'. The Governing and Representative Bodies first met in January 1918, at Westminster, and the Representative Body was incorporated by Royal Charter on 24 April 1919.

One matter of great debate at the Cardiff Convention was the veto of the bishops. Since resolutions and amendments at the Convention had to be approved by a majority in each of the houses of bishops, clergy, and laity, three bishops could ensure the rejection of any proposal. When an amendment was under discussion to reduce the power of the bishops, episcopal rights were forcibly expressed by Archdeacon Green of Monmouth, who declared roundly that 'if this motion is carried I shall take my bag and I shall walk out of the door'. Only 14 out of 362 supported the amendment. Since then the bishops of the Church in Wales have had very great powers within the Church. Another matter which took up a considerable time was whether women could be members of the Governing Body. No

Ecclesiastical Synod had apparently ever had women members. Initially it was decided to allow the Governing Body to co-opt up to twelve women as members. In the event the Governing Body soon allowed women to serve as elected members.

Another topic which roused members of the Convention was that of the number of diocesan representatives to serve on the Governing Body. General agreement obtained that each diocese should be equally represented on the Representative Body, by four clergymen and eight laymen. The Joint Committee's proposal for the Governing Body, however, was that the two more populated southern dioceses should send more members to the Governing Body than the two northern dioceses. But, as Dr. Maurice Jones, then a country parson in Oxfordshire and later Principal of Lampeter, wrote: 'Here again the Convention afforded solid proof of the admirable spirit by which it was governed, and the South Wales delegates responded most readily to the appeal of their brethren from the north that the Diocese, and not population, should be regarded as the unit and that in the matter of representation on the Governing Body every Diocese should be placed on an equality'. Each diocese would therefore elect 25 clergymen and 50 laymen, and all bishops, deans, and archdeacons would be *ex-officio* members. The subsequent creation of two new dioceses in South Wales did, of course, ensure that a majority of members would be from the south.

The Convention also debated the name of the Church. Should it be 'The Church in Wales', 'The Church of Wales', or 'The Welsh Church'? Although most of the speakers favoured 'The Church of Wales', the Welsh Church Act had used the form 'The Church in Wales' and there emerged considerable anxiety as to what might be the legal consequence of adopting a different name. There might be complications in obtaining a Charter of Incorporation for the Representative Body from the Privy Council. The matter was left to the Governing Body, which in 1921 decided on 'The Church in Wales'. Dr. Maurice Jones considered that the Convention's failure to adopt the name of 'The Church of Wales' meant 'the loss of a golden opportunity to make a most effective appeal to the principle and sentiment of nationality and to make a clear and unmistakable declaration of the Church's coming attitude towards the Welsh people in its corporate national capacity'.

All in all Maurice Jones detected a lack of enterprise on the part of the Convention, which had been 'slow to grasp the importance of the "psychological moment" and to realize that now, when hopes are high and hearts are warm, is the time for a bold initiative and not in years to come when hopes may have waned and hearts may have grown cold'. The Convention, depicted by Maurice Jones as made up of delegates from the upper and middle classes, with 'labour' scarcely represented, gave much attention to the word 'Church', but very little to the word 'Wales'. Possibly 'labour' would not have put much stress either on 'Wales' in 1920. Significantly Maurice Jones also noted that the first members of the Governing and Representative Bodies came from the 'same social grades as those who met in the Convention at Cardiff' and he commented: 'It becomes a pertinent question whether a Church whose government is almost entirely in the hands of the upper and middle classes can appeal with any degree of success to Welsh Nonconformists with their markedly democratic leanings or to the teeming thousands in the coalfields and manufacturing districts of South Wales, where the uplifting of labour and hostility to capitalism and all its associations are practically the only religion'. Time would tell.

Nonetheless, whatever the weaknesses of the Convention, by the date of disestablishment the two chief Bodies of the Church were already in existence. Work was also in hand to produce a Constitution for the Church, but it was not until April 1922 that this was completed.

The chief architect of the Constitution was Lord Sankey, to whom the Church in Wales is for ever indebted. As one bishop wrote: '[Sankey] is not only a lawyer, but behind the legal acumen shines the brilliancy of his loyal Churchmanship and his profound and humble reverence for his Lord'. Archbishop Derrick Childs rightly remarked in a lecture in 1983 that 'Holy Trinity Church, Llandrindod Wells, contains inscribed doors as a tangible memorial to Sankey but his real memorial is in the active life and witness of the Church in Wales itself'.

The Governing Body reached a decision on the composition of Diocesan Conferences in January 1918. Each Diocesan Conference would appoint a Diocesan Board of Finance and a Diocesan Board of Patronage. In September of that year the Governing Body discussed the parochial franchise, the tenure of livings, and the election of bishops. There was much animated debate about the franchise for taking part in parochial elections, some suggesting that only regular communicants should be able to vote, others that all confirmed members of the Church should have the vote, and others that all baptized members ought to be able to vote. Ultimately the franchise was given to confirmed members. On the election of bishops a proposal that the Diocesan Conference of the vacant see should elect, with a veto in the hands of the Bench of Bishops, was not accepted. It was agreed instead that the whole Church ought to be involved in the election of a diocesan bishop, with the possibility, later adopted, that the vacant diocese should have additional representation in the electoral college.

(ii) The Bishops and the new Archbishop

The four diocesan bishops of the Church had all been in their episcopal offices for many years before 1920. The Right Reverend Alfred George Edwards, 'gaunt, lean and ascetic-looking' (to quote the late Canon D. Ivor Jones of Monmouth Diocese) had been consecrated Bishop of St. Asaph in 1889, at the age of 40. His episcopate had been tempestuous with controversies inside and outside his diocese. But W. J. Gruffydd might have been exaggerating a little when he described Bishop Edwards as 'the most disastrous man that Wales has ever seen'. The Right Reverend John Owen, 'a very lovable man with a round boyish face, and glasses', had been Bishop of St. Davids since 1897. At 65 years of age he was the youngest bishop in 1920. The Right Reverend Watkin Herbert Williams, 'with his pink cheeks and "mutton chops" looking like a benevolent John Bull', had held the see of Bangor since 1899, while the 'junior bishop', the Right Reverend Joshua Pritchard Hughes of Llandaff had been on the episcopal bench since 1905. He was a 'tall man with a dark beard, and out of doors [he] wore for many years a long black over-coat with a thick Astrakhan collar', reminding Canon Ivor Jones of a Russian nobleman of the old regime. A fifth bishop, the Right Reverend Edward Latham Bevan, had held since 1915 the office of Suffragan Bishop of Swansea, an assistant bishop within the huge Diocese of St. Davids. The Right Reverend Owen Thomas Lloyd Crossley, formerly Bishop of Auckland, New Zealand, served as Assistant Bishop in Llandaff Diocese.

The Bishops in 1920

The Most Reverend C. A. H. Green

The Most Reverend A. G. Edwards

A delightul parody in the *Western Mail* presented a striking picture of the four diocesan bishops, although, as Dr. Chrystal Davies has remarked, 'it did little justice either to the sincerity of Bishop Owen or the seriousness of Bishop Williams':

> The Bishop of St. Asaph,
> Defender of the Right,
> To overcome this evil Bill
> Said, 'Brethren, let us fight'.
> His Lordship from St. Davids,
> With strategic gleam,
> Preliminary to all force,
> Said, 'Brethren, let us scheme'.
> Then Llandaff's noble bishop
> Stood up to have his say:
> 'Before we start to fight or scheme,
> My brethren, let us pray'.
> The three gazed towards Bangor,
> The genial, kind divine;
> He chose his words with wisdom great,
> 'My brethren, let us dine'.

The Bishops of St. Asaph and St. Davids had taken the lead both in fighting disestablishment and in preparing the organizational machinery of the new Church. Although they hoped that the Welsh Bishops might remain members of Convocation, the Parliament of the Church of England, it became clear to them, and to the Archbishop of Canterbury, Randall Davidson, but not at once to the Bishop of Bangor, that it would be impossible to have a Convocation composed of bishops from both an established and a disestablished church, and it was agreed, with much regret and trepidation, that the Church in Wales would have to become a separate Province in ecclesiastical terms, an autonomous Province within the world-wide Anglican Communion, with its own Archbishop. The mother would have to leave the daughter's house. The danger that many feared was that the mother might henceforward be very isolated and lonely.

On 1 April 1920 the Archbishop of Canterbury released the Welsh bishops from their allegiance to him, and on 7 April the bishops met to elect the Archbishop of Wales. Once the Constitution had been completed, the Archbishop would be elected by an Electoral College, made up of bishops, clergy, and laity, but in the election of the first Archbishop the four diocesan bishops would choose one of their number.

The ceremony took place at the Old Parish Church just outside Llandrindod Wells in Radnorshire. Early on a cold and wet morning the bishops, their chaplains and legal officers, and a select number of observers met for Holy Communion, after which Bishop Owen of St. Davids proposed that Bishop Edwards of St. Asaph should be Archbishop. He would, of course, remain Bishop of his diocese. Bishop Edwards was elected unanimously by his three colleagues, and thus he became Archbishop at an age which would already have required his retirement in more recent years. He was to hold his high office for 14 years. On the next day, 8 April, the Governing Body approved the Archbishop's election by acclamation. In a strong address he called on the Church to look forward and not back, and he prophesied that it would be Wales, and not the Church, which would suffer from disestablishment.

On 1 June Archbishop Edwards was enthroned as Archbishop of Wales by the Archbishop of Canterbury in St. Asaph Cathedral. The Archbishop's Chair, a copy in Kentish black oak of St. Augustine's Chair at Canterbury, has subsequently been placed in the cathedral of the diocese of which the Archbishop of Wales has been bishop. The enthronement at St. Asaph was witnessed by a great cloud of witnesses, including Prince Arthur of Connaught, Mr. Lloyd George, the Prime Minister, and the Archbishops of York and Dublin. The Prime Minister later spoke in the pavilion, wishing every blessing to the Church which he had helped to despoil.

3

'The Locust Years': Wales between the Wars

(i) Leadership

The First World War saw tremendous economic growth and massive social changes in Wales. In the countryside the disappearance of most landlords and in the industrial valleys the rise of sharp class consciousness posed many problems. And then in the 1920s and 1930s Wales, rural as well as urban, suffered the agony of what Professor K. O. Morgan has termed 'The Ordeal' of the depression. What was the response of the newly disestablished Church in Wales to these bewildering new conditions?

It might fairly be said that in its first quarter of a century the Church was very cautious. The Governing Body, made up of older clergy and many peers and gentry, was accused of being too ready to follow the path of compromise. Not much change in the social composition of its membership was noticeable until after the Second World War, and even then the change was very limited. Critical contemporaries spoke of the business of the Governing Body being cut and dried, with not enough positive debating. Only the 'top people' spoke at meetings, in English, and many felt that they had little idea of the problems of the ordinary clergy, especially the country clergy, who formed the majority of those serving in the parishes of the Church in Wales. Diocesan Conferences were also dominated by the upper classes.

In a broader sphere allegations were made, with considerable truth, that the Church in Wales was too little involved in the national life of Wales. For example, the Church's members took little part in the National Eisteddfod, although the Archbishop and the Bishop of St. Davids did attend the great festival, and later, in the 1930s, Bishop Havard of St. Asaph was particularly involved in the Eisteddfod.

There were in the 1920s, as later, ordained and lay members of the Church in Wales who were positively hostile to Welsh, regarding it as a second-rate language. Archbishop Edwards himself had a somewhat ambivalent attitude towards Welsh, although, if the story is true, he owed his appointment as Warden of Llandovery College at a young age to knowing the Welsh word for butler. In later life, when he could be very stubborn, he seems to have held up the preparation of an official hymn book in Welsh for the Church in Wales. After he had resigned the work was authorized at once. The Welsh-language press of the Church moved from financial crisis to financial crisis in the 1920s; its position has not, however, improved seventy years later in spite of the much enhanced status of Welsh in our society.

The first task of the Church was to set its house in order, and perhaps no more could have been expected of its leaders. Most of the bishops, higher dignitaries, and leading laymen were well advanced in years. They had all spent long lives in an established church, and they had little idea of how their newly autonomous church ought to develop. The first item on the agenda was to provide the Church in Wales with machinery for its governance. In December 1920 Frank Morgan, Secretary of the Governing and Representative Bodies, listed items for discussion—the division of dioceses, the amalgamation of benefices, a central examination for ordinands, a clergy superannuation scheme, tribunals, and the problem of episcopal palaces. Another great need was to seek to create an esprit de corps among the Church's members, in particular to lead those from North Wales and those from South Wales into a common mind. Clergy and laity could, on the whole, identify with their dioceses; identifying with a new Province would be much more difficult. Perhaps such identification is only beginning to show itself after seventy years.

Archbishop Edwards went on a progress through South Wales in 1921 to meet the members of the Church in places far distant from St. Asaph and to listen to their problems, but he had been a bishop for over 30 years and it was difficult for him to change his accustomed ways. Historians have speculated that things might have been very different if the younger Bishop Owen of St. Davids had been elected Archbishop. But Archbishop Edwards was to be around for a long time; indeed he was to be Archbishop until after all the other diocesan bishops of 1920 had resigned or died.

New bishops were elected to Monmouth in 1921 and to Swansea and Brecon in 1923, as we shall see later, but the first change of diocesan bishop came in Bangor in 1925, after the retirement of Bishop Williams, who survived, however, to live into his hundredth year. His successor was the Right Reverend Daniel Davies. Bishop John Owen of St. Davids died in 1926, and was succeeded by the Right Reverend David Lewis Prosser, previously Archdeacon of St. Davids. The sudden death of Bishop Davies of Bangor in 1928 led to the translation to Bangor of the Right Reverend Charles Alfred Howell Green, Bishop of Monmouth since 1921, and the new Bishop of Monmouth was the Right Reverend Gilbert Cunningham Joyce, previously, like Dr. Prosser, Archdeacon of St. Davids, and before that Principal of St. David's College, Lampeter. In 1931 Bishop Hughes of Llandaff died, and he was succeeded by the Right Reverend Timothy Rees, an Anglican monk of the Community of the Resurrection at Mirfield. But in spite of often feeling despondent, Archbishop Edwards remained Archbishop and Bishop of St. Asaph until 1934, when he had reached his 86th year. From 1928 he had the assistance of the Right Reverend Thomas Lloyd, styled Bishop of Maenan and consecrated at the age of 70, as his suffragan in St. Asaph, Bishop Lloyd was the only assistant bishop in the disestablished Church in Wales to be granted a territorial title, Maenan being a pre-Reformation abbey in the Conwy Valley.

While the bishops provided, or might be expected to provide, spiritual leadership in the Church in Wales, no account of the early years could be complete without a reference to Mr. Frank Morgan. Mr. Morgan had been a Fellow of Keble College, Oxford, until he was prevailed upon in 1918 to become the chief lay executive of the Church in Wales. In spite of misunderstandings, leading more than once to the threat of resignation from his office, he worked in reasonable harmony with Archbishop Edwards and Bishop Owen, each of whom had been his Headmaster at Llandovery College, and Frank Morgan, more than anyone else, settled the administration of the Church on firm foundations. At one time he served as secretary of 30 Church committees, including the Governing and Representative Bodies, and also as Archbishop's Registrar. His dedication was such that in 1931 he took a cut in salary to help the uncertain finances of the Church. Frank Morgan had an astonishing knowledge of the parishes and clergy of the Church in Wales; he died in its service on 22 December 1935.

The story of the episcopate and of the Governing Body during these years is, on the whole, one of timidity and caution. Some individuals did, however, exercise notable ministries. For example, Bishop Timothy Rees spoke in his enthronement sermon at Llandaff of his desire to help the 'broken lives and broken hearts that are the result of this depression'. He initiated direct relief and served as chairman of the Llandaff Industrial Committee. The Industrial Christian Fellowship Crusade to the Rhondda in 1938, undertaken at the Bishop's suggestion, strengthened the morale of the clergy and the laity in that ravaged part of Wales.

(ii) Financial Problems

During these grim 'locust years' between the Wars Wales suffered mass unemployment and immense poverty, in rural as well as in industrial areas. Emigration, especially from South Wales, took away many young and able people. It was not a propitious time for setting up a new ecclesiastical organization. Contemporaries were already speaking, moreover, of 'pagan Wales', in which Christianity appeared to be no more than 'an amusing hobby' for many of its adherents. Clearly the challenges to the Church were many, but for a long time the Church in Wales, perhaps inevitably, found itself preoccupied with its own problems, mainly financial and legal. The Governing Body did, however, contribute to the National Fund for the relief of distress in the coalfields in 1928, and we have already noted Bishop Timothy Rees's work.

It appears, nonetheless, that of much more immediate concern to the leaders of the Church were the financial difficulties they faced. An Appeal to raise £1 million, to provide an income of about £48,000 a year to make up for the losses of disendowment, had produced £661,730 by 1923, and ultimately it was closed in about 1935 when £722,552 had been raised, not a trivial sum in the conditions. There were fewer landlords to contribute money, although Henry Gladstone of Hawarden gave the handsome sum of £20,000. The Church of England had been very voluble before disestablishment in promising financial assistance to its sister Church, but little cash ever actually arrived from across the border. Nonetheless, by 1937 it was generally felt, and rightly so, that the financial condition of the Church in Wales was as sound as it had been before disestablishment—although even then it had been

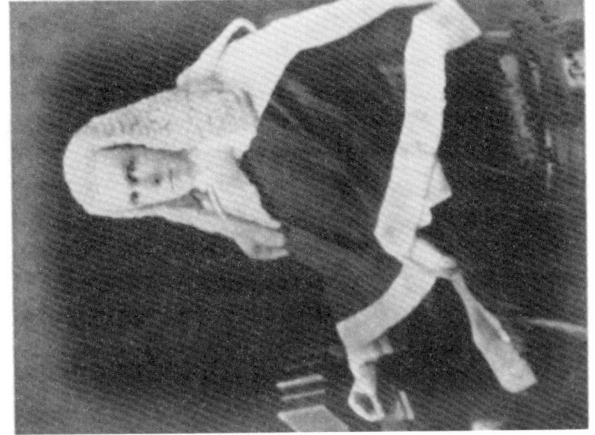

Judge Sankey

Mr. Frank Morgan

St. George, Rhos-on-Sea (St. Asaph)
(1913, tower completed 1965)

D. T. W. Price

St. Julius and St. Aaron, Newport (Monmouth)
(consecrated 1926)

D. R. Williams

poorer than the Church of England. Most of the income of the Church went to pay clerical stipends, now on a standard scale, except for those clergymen who had been in their existing posts in 1914.

The Governing Body spent much of its time discussing domestic matters during its twice-yearly meetings at Llandrindod, a town which was equally inconvenient of access for almost all members, from North and South, but which was well endowed with hotels. The Governing Body's procedure was generally slow, but some issues were approved quite quickly. The name of the Church was settled in 1921. By 1922 the Constitution was completed. A full analysis of it may be found in C. A. H. Green, *The Setting of the Constitution of the Church in Wales* (1937). Later topics of debate included the establishment of rules for administering the cathedrals in the changed circumstances after disestablishment, the Church press, especially in Welsh, Sunday Schools, the grouping of country parishes to save stipends, pensions for clergy and clergy widows, marriage legislation, churchyards, curates' pay, the problem of the post-Confirmation child, and the maintenance and repair of clergy houses. Virtually no attention was given to liturgical, ecumenical, or social issues. Little success attended a proposal that each diocese ought to have a full-time Religious Education adviser and a diocesan missioner, although diocesan missioners did, it seems, work in Llandaff and Swansea & Brecon Dioceses for several years. The publication in 1924 of the first *Year Book* of the Church in Wales, provided free of charge to the clergy, did much to develop some sense of provincial awareness, very necessary in a Church in which primary loyalties were to one of the 'six kingdoms', the six dioceses, while the creation of a Provincial Board of Patronage in 1927 was intended to assist clergy in moving between dioceses.

A Training Committee for Ordinands had been established in 1920, just before the date of disestablishment, and in the early 1920s fears were already being expressed about the inadequate number of ordinands and about the considerable number of middle-aged candidates for ordination, although by the standards of the 1980s the problem scarcely looks serious. By the late 1920s numbers had picked up considerably, largely thanks to the existence of St. David's College, Lampeter and of St. Michael's College, Llandaff, which provided sound courses for ordination at a moderate cost, with many scholarships and bursaries to help those from poorer homes.

(iii) New Dioceses and Liturgy

In one respect, however, the Church in Wales showed considerable courage, and this was in the creation of two new dioceses. There had long been a general, possibly unanimous, feeling that the Diocese of Llandaff was too large in population. Its eastern part, almost coterminous with the county of Monmouthshire, became the new Diocese of Monmouth in 1921, with the Right Reverend Charles Green, previously Archdeacon of Monmouth, as its first bishop. Local laymen gave generously towards the stipend of the Bishop. St. Woolos's Church in Newport became the pro-cathedral, and in 1930 a Chapter was set up there. On 29 September 1949 the Governing Body agreed to St. Woolos's becoming the cathedral of the diocese.

More doubt seems to have been felt about the division of the largest diocese in area, that of St. Davids. Proposals to divide it into at least three dioceses—Brecon, St. Davids, and Swansea—came to nothing, but by 1923 there was sufficient approval for the creation of the new Diocese of Swansea and Brecon, to include Breconshire, most of Radnorshire, the Swansea Valley, and Gower. Bishop Bevan, Suffragan Bishop of Swansea, had long been in effect Bishop in Breconshire and Radnorshire, and he raised £8,660 in two months to endow the new bishopric. He was the obvious man to be the first Bishop of Swansea and Brecon, and he was so elected, but he was enthroned only after the Archbishop had made the gesture of not confirming his appointment on the grounds that he did not speak Welsh. Bishop Bevan was the first bishop appointed in Wales since 1870 not to have at least some knowledge of Welsh.

After the decision had been taken to set up the Diocese of Swansea and Brecon one commentator noted that it would be twenty years before another new diocese could be established. In fact no new diocese has been created since 1923. Raising clerical stipends took precedence over establishing new dioceses. But movements of population were met, to a limited extent, by the building of new churches and the creation of new parishes, especially in the Dioceses of Llandaff and Monmouth, with many of the new churches being temporary structures. To pay the incumbents of these new parishes small country parishes were amalgamated, the Governing Body having agreed in 1925 to the grouping of 40 tiny rural livings.

The middle years of the 1920s witnessed much debate about the worship of the Church of England, with a new alternative Prayer Book (the 'Deposited Book') being accepted by the Church in 1927 and 1928, only to be rejected by Parliament. Some Welsh clergy would have liked to have seen a new Prayer Book for the Church in Wales, but there was no support for this among the bishops. After all the Church in Wales had not wished to be separated from the Church of England, and many in Wales were perfectly happy with the 1662 *Book of Common Prayer*. Some clergy, nonetheless, appear to have been attracted to the new English Prayer Book of 1928. It was left to the Welsh bishops to consider whether or not to authorize the 1928 book in Wales. They did not make any formal announcement, but borrowing from the 1928 book happened on a relatively large scale. In some Anglo-Catholic parishes, especially in Cardiff, borrowing from more exotic liturgies was not unknown.

Officially, of course, the Church in Wales's sole legal *Book of Common Prayer* remained that of 1662, with the phrase 'according to the use of the Church of England' still printed on the title page. The Church in Wales had the right to alter its worship and to produce a new Prayer Book, as the Constitution declared: 'The Governing Body shall have power to make alterations in...rites, ceremonies, and formularies...by a Bill...backed and introduced in the Governing Body by a majority of the Order of the Bishops'. The conservatism of the Church in Wales, especially of its bishops and laity, however, kept the 1662 *Book of Common Prayer* as the only official Prayer Book until the 1950s, when experimental services of Baptism and Confirmation were introduced.

In one uncontroversial but interesting respect the Church in Wales did acknowledge its separate existence from the Church of England. In 1936 the Governing Body requested the Bench of Bishops to make proposals for a Calendar of Welsh Saints. The Calendar was adopted in 1944. It indicated the days on which a number of Welsh saints could be commemorated, although it provided no collects or readings for these occasions. Most, perhaps all, bishops did, however, authorize a collect and readings for the feast of St. David.

(iv) Missions and Ecumenism

Brave efforts were made, right from 1920, to remind Welsh Anglicans of the needs of the missions overseas. The Church in

Wales had no official missionary society of its own, but parishes contributed to the work of the well-known missionary societies of the Church of England, such as the Church Missionary Society and the Society for the Propagation of the Gospel. From time to time bishops from other parts of the Anglican Communion visited Wales to remind the members of the Church in Wales of their existence and needs. A Missionary Council of the Church in Wales, set up by the Governing Body in 1922, was never very effective.

The members of the Church in Wales needed less reminding of the other Christians in their midst, the Nonconformists, to use a word which continued to be employed to describe the Protestant denominations. The years immediately after disestablishment were not the time for serious attempts at unity with those who had 'despoiled and robbed' the Anglican Church, and there was considerable resistance to attempts to work together. The Committee for Mutual Co-operation and Understanding between Christian Communions in Wales, established in 1930, did little. The Nonconformist Churches, now losing members, still saw the Church in Wales as too English in its outlook, and the field for the most determined co-operation, that of religious education in schools, produced little result.

The Church in Wales, shaken after disestablishment, laid great stress on its being the National and Catholic Church in Wales. Lord Sankey expressed the feelings of many when he spoke after the acceptance of the Constitution in April 1922: 'That, Ladies and Gentlemen, completed the Constitution of the Church in Wales . . . We do not stand alone. The Church in Wales is a Catholic and National Church. As a Catholic Church you are not at liberty to consult your own desires or to do as you like. You are a branch of the great Catholic and Apostolic Church, with explicit creeds and determined traditions. See to it then, that you discount innovations which may impair your own communion with others. As a national church we are the old Christian Church in these islands. The saints of the Church of God are sons of the race. They sleep in Welsh soil, hard by the shrines they loved and served so well. The self-same prayers which moved their lips move ours. Today we are the heirs of their beliefs and of their traditions. You stand now, strong and united. See to it you do not imperil that newly found strength and unity . . . Give me leave in my last words to recall that the Church in Wales is the Church of Christ. Let us listen for the faintest whisper of His voice. To know what He wishes and to obey what He commands is the one sure salvation for our country and ourselves'.

One perceptive scholar, the Reverend Canon David Walker, has seen the history of the Church in Wales since 1920 as the gradual integration, after the alienation of the eighteenth century, of the Church into Welsh society. It must be said that there was little integration during the first quarter of a century of the Church's independent life, although perhaps one might rightly see these years as a period when the essential foundations were laid for the subsequent undoubted integration of the Church into Welsh life.

Inevitably during these years, and indeed in later years also, many Churchpeople in Wales looked to the past with nostalgia. A distinguished layman and convert from Nonconformity, Mr. Aneirin Talfan Davies, still considered in the early 1950s that the Church in Wales was 'like a people who have been left in an open boat, casting longing eyes at the liner which we have just left, feeling a little despondent in the desert of sea around us'. He continued: 'It will take some time before we get our bearings right, and realize that from henceforth we shall have to row our own boat'. Archbishop Green, however, considered at the Church Congress in Bournemouth in 1935 that disestablishment had been a blessing to the Church in Wales.

If the Church in Wales had gained from disestablishment, ought the Church of England to be disestablished also? The editor of *Crockford's Clerical Directory* commented: 'It is no doubt true that if a certain traveller had completed his journey without molestation the Good Samaritan might never had the opportunity of exhibiting his admirable qualities. But we are quite unable to assent to any exegesis of that parable which would see in it an abstract justification of highway robbery with violence'.

4

'New Life': 1945-1968

(i) Commissions and Committees

The Church emerged from the Second World War with a bombed Cathedral and Theological College at Llandaff and several bombed churches in Cardiff and Swansea. Financial problems were as acute as those in 1920, partly as a result of government financial policy during the War, but the sense of being in a new world after 1945 soon showed itself in the setting up of several important Commissions and Committees. The godly and eirenic Archbishop Prosser, Bishop of St. Davids, had succeeded Archbishop Green in 1944, apparently after the Archiepiscopal Electoral College had reached a deadlock on whether to choose Bishop John Morgan of Llandaff or Bishop William Havard of St. Asaph.

Furthermore, the biographer of Archbishop Edwards felt after the War that 'a new spirit is abroad, and all the old asperities have gone. The Welsh Church is more closely allied to all the Welsh national institutions, and the vicar of an upland parish in Denbighshire has been crowned at the National Eisteddfod for his contribution to Welsh poetry. The leaders of the Welsh Church—clerical and lay—are held in respect and regard, and in the new atmosphere created in the past quarter of a century lies the hope that the vision of ultimate reunion may brighten as the days pass'. The tide had begun to turn, but much still had to be done to bring the Church in Wales fully into national life and to establish closer relations with the other churches in Wales. The Church's financial problems, apparently a surprise to many, who thought that it was still relatively affluent, as it had been in 1939, led to the setting up of a new Reconstruction Committee in 1945. This had the task of discovering how clerical stipends could be increased through the grouping of parishes. In 1946 a Commission

The Most Reverend John Morgan

The Most Reverend D. L. Prosser

St. David, Hundleton (St. Davids)
(consecrated 1934)

N. Pearce

St. Peter, Penrhosgarnedd (Bangor)
(consecrated 1957)

R. M. Keating

on Religious Education in Wales was set up, and its Report, over 80 pages in length and presented to the Governing Body in September 1947, revealed a keen awareness of the 'unparalleled educational opportunities' of the time. It contained bold and constructive proposals. The Report made valuable suggestions on improving religious teaching in Schools after the 1944 Education Act, on Sunday Schools, which were very unsatisfactory, on Adult Religious Education, and on the work of the Church in the University and the training colleges. A Provincial Council for Education, with five sub-committees, was created to watch over all aspects of the Church's educational activities, and diocesan councils of education also appeared, but financial constraints limited the actual work of many dedicated educationalists. In 1947 the Commission on the Nation and Prayer Book was brought into being, and its important Report of 1949 will be considered in greater detail below. In 1948 a Commission on Cathedrals attempted once again to tackle the difficult problem of how cathedrals were to be staffed and financed.

There had been so much activity since 1945 that by 1949 the new Archbishop, the Most Reverend John Morgan, Bishop of Llandaff, was appealing, unsuccessfully, for a respite in the number of new committees and commissions, and for a 'Holy Year', so that every member of the Church in Wales could be free to get on with the work of evangelization, although it is reasonable to hope that committees also may be instruments for spreading the Gospel. By 1951 there was also a Provincial Evangelistic Council. But the Church did more at this time than set up committees; mention should be made of the Mission to Cardiff in 1952 and of the Welsh Church Congress in Llandrindod Wells in 1953. Above all much enthusiasm was evident in the work of Cymry'r Groes, the youth organization, planned from 1942 and in being by 1944. Hundreds of young people found their faith and commitment deepened through this imaginative venture. Its Pilgrimage to St. Davids in 1955 was outstanding. The Anglican Young People's Association also made a significant contribution.

The Commission known as that on the Nation and Prayer Book had originally been established by the Bench of Bishops in April 1947 to consider 'what reforms might be made to put the Church in a better position to take a larger part in the life of the nation, and in particular, as preparation for a possible revision of the Book of Common Prayer, to report upon

(1) The present position in Canon Law as to the Prayer Book and Lectionary.

(2) The various revisions of the Prayer Book which have been undertaken in other Provinces of the Church'.

The findings of the Commission, reported to the Governing Body in September 1949, were not encouraging. The Church in Wales had not been in the forefront of theological thinking in Wales for over a century, and a revival of theology was essential for the future health of Welsh Christianity. Preaching needed to be more effective too. In facing the developments in Welsh society since 1920 members of the Church in Wales were not sufficiently aware of the problems of Wales as a whole. They were too confined in their interests to their own parishes. But the members of the Commission were sure that there were many opportunities for the Church, as the Church, to make a fuller contribution to national life, especially in the arts and in education.

Pastoral problems in the countryside were examined, and it was noted that 'the continuous prosperity of the agricultural community since the late thirties, a prosperity in sharp contrast with the hardships of the immediately preceding period' had weakened the natural sense of religion in the rural areas. The decline in the number of ordinands from rural districts made for difficulties when town-bred clergy moved into ministry in the countryside. Perhaps large-scale grouping of parishes around small towns or large villages would be a more effective use of manpower. As far as industrial areas were concerned there was great indifference and religious ignorance, and everywhere the parochial system needed drastic overhauling. The problems were clearly stated; implementing remedies was not to be so easy.

Much space was given in the Report to the Welsh language and the Welsh way of life, and it was felt 'that the Welsh way of life does not enter as widely and naturally as it should do into the life of the Church'. There were parishes in which Welsh was vigorous, but for the most part 'in Welsh-speaking Wales the Church is widely held to be isolated from Welsh life'. The Church could do much more to welcome and encourage Welsh speakers. At a higher level the Church, unlike some of the Nonconformist denominations, seldom made pronouncements on matters of concern to Wales in general. The same criticism, that the Church was withdrawn from the main currents of national life, could be made of the Church's contribution to Welsh academic and intellectual life. It would take a long time to rectify this isolation, which extended to arts and crafts also. One wonders whether much progress has even yet been made in this matter, apart from the work of a few individuals.

When the Report turned to Wales and the Book of Common Prayer it declared: 'It is widely felt that we have reached a position in which practical and pastoral needs require both the amendment and enrichment of our present Prayer Book [that of 1662] in certain directions, and a greater degree of authoritative direction in respect of the many and various practices and customs associated with parochial worship'. The members of the Commission suggested two principles for the Governing Body's consideration. The first was that 'a beginning should be made with such changes in the existing Prayer Book as are required by pastoral and practical considerations' and the second was that 'no attempt should be made at any large scale revision at any one time; rather, such changes as may be desirable and generally acceptable should be authorised in stages'. The authors of the Report further requested the Archbishop to appoint a Commission, to be known as the Standing Liturgical Commission, to advice the Bench of Bishops on possible changes to the Church's law of worship.

The Standing Liturgical Commission was established in January 1951. It began its work by circulating a questionnaire on liturgical practice to every incumbent in the Province. The Commission's brief was to advise the bishops, and liturgical revision has been a delicate matter in so far as the relationship between the Bench of Bishops and the Governing Body has been concerned. The Commission sent its opinions to the bishops. If they approved changes they took them to the Governing Body. If the Governing Body accepted the proposed services they were then permitted to be used experimentally in each diocese if its bishop gave permission.

It was a slow process, perhaps too slow, but very gradually the Church in Wales took its part in the general revision of liturgies within the Anglican Communion, a revision in the light of theological, historical, sociological, and liturgical scholarship. In September 1956 the Governing Body approved the experimental use of a revised Table of Lessons and Psalms for Sundays and certain other days. Revision of services began with the occasional offices. The first new experimental services were those for Infant and Adult Baptism—in which the optional use of a white vesture and a lighted candle was introduced—and for Confirmation, approved by each bishop for use in his diocese from 1 January 1958 for ten years. Revised Marriage and Churching services followed in 1960. Further liturgical revision will be noted later in this account.

An important new venture after the War was the establishment of the Historical Society of the Church in Wales, following the depositing of the Church's records in the National Library of Wales at Aberystwyth. The Society organized lectures at a national level, and for some time there were also diocesan lectures in Llandaff and St. Davids. The first issue of many of the superb *Journal* of the Society appeared in 1947.

(ii) Finance and Clerical Manpower

But all the activities of the Church were gravely handicapped by a lack of finance and by an increasing shortage of clergy. In a contemporary biannual magazine called *Pan-Anglican*, published in the U.S.A. and intended to make the various Churches of the Anglican Communion better known to one another, the Archbishop of Wales introduced the special Church in Wales issue in October 1952 with the confession that 'we in Wales need many friends, because we are passing through years more trying than any we have yet encountered since we became a separate province'. He hastened to add: 'I do not wish to suggest that the Church in Wales is losing heart and courage... While nothing spectacular is being done, we can claim that the real work of the Church is going on steadily. But the firmest believer and the hardiest fighter like to be assured that they are not alone; they find comfort in knowing that there are other like-minded people, doing much the same work, who, though often far away, are joined to them by bonds of real friendship'.

The serious problems of finance and manpower were closely related. Clerical stipends had scarcely been increased since 1939, and in real terms they were worth less than half what they had been before the Second World War. Clergy, especially curates, and more especially curates with wives and children, frequently succumbed to the better stipends of the Church of England, which also provided free housing for curates, and some clergy felt obliged to leave the parochial ministry altogether and to take up other work, usually in teaching. The loss of Welsh-speaking curates was a particularly serious problem. The financial condition of the clergy did not attract many ordinands, and it became necessary to group more and more country parishes, although on looking back from 1990 we observe that there was still a remarkable number of single-church rural parishes in Wales even at the end of the 1950s. It was well-nigh impossible to establish specialist ministries— industrial, agricultural, hospital, or educational chaplaincies—or to provide residential canonries in the cathedrals for scholars. Perhaps the failure to establish specialist non-parochial ministries had more than financial reasons; the Governing Body showed opposition to specialist ministries as late as the 1960s. Some expansion of the traditional parochial ministry was a different matter. For example, thirteen new churches in Monmouth Diocese were built and staffed between 1945 and 1962.

A great deal of the income of the Church came from the Provincial Levy or Quota, an annual contribution to the central finances of the Church from each parish, although such 'live giving' accounted for less than half the Church's income, the remainder coming from invested endowments. Year by year the Quota had to be raised to permit a modest increase in clerical stipends and pensions, but the slow inflation of the late 1940s and early 1950s left clerical incomes in an ever more parlous state in real terms.

At the Governing Body meeting of September 1949 the lay members met together, for the first time ever without the clergy, to discuss how clerical stipends could be raised, and the result was the Laymen's Appeal of 1952, a great boost to morale. The target was £½ million, to be raised from the parishes in addition to the Quota; by the summer of 1953 the target had been exceeded. Clerical stipends had actually already been increased in faith by using reserves in anticipation of the success of the Laymen's Appeal. By 1954 the Quota stood at £145,000 a year, only £51,000 less than that of the Church of England, which had fourteen times as many parishes as the Church in Wales. At the end of 1954 the old gilt edged policy was abandoned in favour of a limited investment in equities. The Representative Body was empowered to invest a much larger proportion than hitherto of capital in non-trustee securities. Bush House was purchased in February 1955 for £2½ million; it was sold in 1972 for £22 million. This was part of the great work of the Finance Committee of the Representative Body, chaired by Mr. D. M. Vaughan, known for his financial expertise. He never failed to acknowledge the help given to him by Mr. W. R. Jones, the accountant of the Representative Body. In 1962 Sir David James gave the Church £204,000 over six years on condition that the Church raised an equivalent amount, as it did.

But the number of ordinands did not grow, and the clerical exodus to England continued apace. Perhaps shortage of finance was not the only reason for the lack of ordinands; the conservatism of the Church in Wales's elderly leaders and possibly the lack of specialist ministries in Wales led many young men to cross over to England, where stipends were also higher. The editor of *Crockford's Clerical Directory* could not resist commenting in 1946 that 'after twenty-five years' experience of the blessings of freedom from State interference Welsh clergy are not reluctant to accept work in England' and again in 1954 in the context of Welsh migration to England that 'not a few parsons seem to prefer the shackles of an Established Church to the "freedom" which some within it seem to desire'. Between 1947 and 1954 276 priests left Wales for England; it was estimated in the latter year that 600 priests ordained in Wales were then serving in England. The movement was not reciprocal. In 1962 700 priests ordained in Wales were serving in England, but only ten priests ordained in England were ministering in Wales.

In the late 1930s the Church in Wales had 981 incumbents, 476 curates, and 1,750 churches. To maintain clerical numbers it would be necessary after the War to ordain 70 deacons a year, but only 163 were ordained between 1947 and 1952. Half the curacies were vacant; in due course half the benefices might also be. A Governing Body Commission on Manpower produced an unsatisfactory Report, and the vital matter of ordination candidates was left to the dioceses.

(iii) Leadership and Liturgy

Following the death of Archbishop John Morgan in 1957 Welsh clergymen did not have to leave Wales to serve under an English Archbishop, since the new Archbishop of Wales was the Most Reverend Alfred Edwin Morris, Bishop of Monmouth. Archbishop Morris was a native of Worcestershire, but he had followed a brilliant academic career at school and college in Lampeter. He became Professor of Hebrew and Theology at Lampeter in 1923 a few weeks after graduating at Oxford, and he remained at St. David's College until his election to the Diocese of Monmouth in 1945. The election of an Englishman, even one who was senior Bishop in Wales, to the Primacy of the Church in Wales led to considerable public controversy, although perhaps awareness of Welshness was less in 1957 than it would be later.

To many zealous Welsh speakers the election of an Englishman confirmed their worst suspicions of the Church in Wales being, in spite of its disestablishment, still an alien Church, the English Mission in their midst. The distinguished poet Gwenallt left the Church in protest against its anglicizing. Bishop Glyn Simon of Llandaff wrote in his *Diocesan Leaflet* about the election of Archbishop Morris and that of Bishop John Thomas, who did not speak Welsh, to Swansea and Brecon as 'a severe blow to the confidence of many Welsh-speaking Church folk'. He added that 'these recent elections, and utterances both before and after them, have revealed an anti-Welsh and pro-English trend, and, in some cases, a bigotry as narrow and ill-informed as any to be found in the tightest, and most remote of Welsh communities'. Bishop Gwilym Williams of Bangor wrote of 'the ambiguous attitude of our Church to the Welsh language'.

Archbishop Morris remained Archbishop of Wales until his retirement in 1968, 'a living refutation of the argument that election produces mediocrity' according to the editor of *Crockford*. As John Peart-Binns has written: 'The Welsh language controversy recurred at frequent intervals during Morris's archiepiscopate. He loved the land that became his, serving and giving much to it. But aspects of the Welsh dimension were missing'. Archbishop Morris's views on alcohol and Sunday observance, and his statement that the Church in Wales was the 'Catholic Church in this land', with all other denominations being 'intruders' (the word used by Morris, which wounded very deeply for many years) were clearly and logically developed, but perhaps a Welshman would not have expressed himself in quite the same way. Nonetheless, not to have elected Bishop Morris Archbishop would have been unacceptable to many, probably the majority of, Welsh Anglicans, for it would have been a signal that only a bilingual bishop could be elected archbishop, and it would have made the archbishopric the monopoly of the minority of clergy who spoke Welsh. There seems to be a fundamental law that it is impossible to please all the inhabitants of Wales, whatever is done.

During Archbishop Morris's tenure of the Primacy liturgical revision pressed steadily ahead. By 1965 revised versions of the Lectionary and of the services of Baptism, Confirmation, Churching, Marriage, and Burial were in use. And in September 1966 the Governing Body approved an experimental version of the Holy Eucharist, a form of service which won high praise from liturgists throughout the world. It was first used at a meeting of the Governing Body on 5 April 1967. The Holy Communion service in the 1662 *Book of Common Prayer* continued, of course, to be a legal rite in Wales.

Also during these years the beginnings of pastoral reorganization were seen with the creation of some Rectorial Benefices, usually the grouping of several urban parishes under a team of clergy, headed by a rector, assisted by vicars and curates. Another reform of Archbishop Morris's time was the introduction of compulsory clerical retirement at the age of 70 years, a controversial matter which aggravated the problem of the shortage of active priests. It is ironic that twenty years later the parochial system survives in some parts of Wales only because retired clergymen, some unwillingly deprived of their own parishes at the age of 70, give so freely of their services on Sundays.

Bishop Glyn Simon painted a bleak, yet accurate, picture of the Church in Wales when he preached to the Governing Body in September 1964 on the text 'It is enough for you to have my grace: it is in weakness that my power is truly felt' (2 Corinthians, 9, v.12 [Moffat's Translation]). He underlined the statistical weakness of the Church: 'Less than ten per cent of the people of Wales are amongst our Easter Communicants. This is substantially less than thirty or forty years ago. Four hundred fewer clergy are serving the Province than were doing so at that date. Twenty-five years ago there were nearly three hundred men in training for the ministry at all levels; to-day there are less than a hundred [an under-estimate]. There are parishes in my diocese where one per cent or less have any serious connection with any kind of organised religion'. He continued in unforgettable language: 'It is said that things are better in the rural areas. But I know large tracts of rural Wales where there seems to be something approaching spiritual death brooding over vicarage and parish alike; it is "like people, like priest"'. The need was for 'more holy bishops, more holy priests, more holy men and women', and for a membership which would give so generously that that there would be no financial difficulty at all, so that the Church could attempt 'vitalising experiments and adventures, which keep us from stagnation, and which, even if they fail, preserve us from complacency or an attitude of helplessly waiting upon events'. But because he believed 'that the Spirit of God can reinvigorate and reinspire his Church in Wales' Glyn Simon was, in spite of much that could discourage, full of hope.

5

'Growth into Maturity': 1968-1990

(i) Leadership

When Archbishop Morris retired in 1968 the senior bishop was the Right Reverend David Daniel Bartlett, Bishop of St. Asaph. If precedent had been followed he would have been elected sixth Archbishop of Wales, although he was then aged 68 and he would have to retire, under a new rule, at the age of 70. One also doubts that Bishop Bartlett would have wished to become Archbishop at his age, or perhaps at any time. In the event he was not given the opportunity, for the Right Reverend William Glyn Hughes Simon, Bishop of Llandaff, was elected Archbishop.

Glyn Simon was one of the few Welsh bishops widely known outside Wales. According to the editor of *Crockford*, he 'won the respect of churchpeople outside as well as within Wales for his humility and his clear, fresh understanding of the spiritual issues in secular life'. Not everyone liked him, but he certainly could not be ignored. In his earlier years he had been a powerful influence on the ordinands in his charge first at the Church Hostel in Bangor and then at St. Michael's College in Llandaff. After holding the deanery of Llandaff he was consecrated Bishop of Swansea and Brecon in 1954 and then translated to Llandaff in 1957. We have noted his public misgivings about the election of Archbishop Morris in 1957; we turn now to consider his archiepiscopate. Simon held the archbishopric for only three years, before he was obliged to resign because of Parkinson's Disease, but in those years, building upon his work as a diocesan bishop during many years, he fixed the Church in Wales firmly within the context of Welsh society.

Since Simon's time, and with the decisive and sensitive work of his successors in the archbishopric, it has surely been impossible to regard the Church in Wales as 'an alien church'. It would be a

The Most Reverend W. G. H. Simon

The Most Reverend A. E. Morris

All Souls, Tycoch (Swansea and Brecon)
(dedicated 1957)   *R. Britton*

St. John Baptist, Ystradyfodwg (Llandaff)
(consecrated 1987)   *P. N. Coleman*

delusion to describe it as the Church *of* Wales or the Church of the Welsh people, for Wales is Christian now in little more than name, but inasmuch as any Christian leader may be seen by 1990 as the leading representative of Christianity in Wales—Welsh-speaking Wales *and* English-speaking Wales—that leader must be the Archbishop of Wales in the Church in Wales. Glyn Simon set that pattern.

In September 1968 he addressed the Governing Body on Wales and the Welsh language. He sketched the religious background to modern Wales, with a useful, if overdrawn, picture of past Nonconformist supremacy in Wales. Nonconformity 'imposed on Wales a pattern known as "the Welsh way of life"', by which must be understood life as lived in pious Nonconformist homes, puritan, protestant, teetotal, sabbatarian and Welsh-speaking. In this way walked until recently the great majority of the professors, bank-managers, doctors, teachers, members of Parliament, county councillors, trades union leaders, substantial farmers and shopkeepers of Wales, as well as the great Welsh drapers and milk retailers of London. Over against them stood the old Church of the land, the Church of an aristocracy and gentry completely English in upbringing and outlook, the Church of the great English immigration that industrialization brought to Wales, but also still the Church of a Welsh-speaking minority which included scholarly Welsh clerics who kept alive the Welsh literary tradition in the days when the Methodists thought nothing of it; the Church, too, of the poor and the feckless, so seldom at home with puritans'.

'Now', he continued, 'the pattern is changing; the decline of nonconformity is marked; there is respect and even affection for the now disestablished Church'. The Church, like Nonconformity, faced a crisis. The world, including Wales, was experiencing a revived national spirit, and 'there is nothing unscriptural or un-Christian in nationalism as such'. Wales was a nation, not a region, but a nation with much disunity and many quarrels. Language divided its people, and the Church, which had not contributed sufficiently to Welsh-speaking society, had to become 'a truly bilingual Church'.

He concluded: 'Let me end by saying once again that we are in Wales today in a potentially dangerous situation and that in such a situation the Church has a specially responsible ministry of reconciliation. Let her show herself to be a Church of understanding and sympathy for *all* her children. Let those who speak English only have a special and Christian care for the rights and grievances of the Welsh-speaking minority; let those who speak Welsh only, or from choice, remember that majorities, too, have rights and grievances which deserve to be respected'.

During his brief tenure of the Archbishopric Glyn Simon, driven by a strong sense of urgency for himself and for the Church, sought to live up to his own words, and, as the most distinguished historian of the Church in Wales, Archdeacon Owain Jones, has commented: 'By his sympathetic awareness of the many facets of Welsh life he became truly "Archbishop of Wales" and a spokesman for the Principality'. Dr. Pennar Davies, a noted member of the Union of Welsh Independents (or Congregationalists), could write in 1972: 'I hope that most Welsh "churchmen" find Glyn Simon's contribution to a Welsh *aggiornamento* as encouraging as I do'.

Not all Anglicans approved of some of his actions, for example, his visiting of Dafydd Iwan in prison and his support for the Welsh language and Welsh culture. But as an article in the short-lived periodical *Impact* put it: 'The Archiepiscopate now ended has been marked by a turning towards Wales, its people and its problems: and there has been a consequential returned affection for the Archbishop by Welsh Christians, both "Free" and "Roman" and amongst non-christians who could find in Dr. Simon a spokesman so patently not "of the establishment" that new and perhaps permanent links have been forged. His speeches and sermons, spoken in his quiet manner, have always shown a grave concern for the problems of Wales. Always declaring that there was no prophet in the land, he never-the-less foresaw the effects of the recession in the coal industry in South Wales, he warned against monolithic employment in the steel industries and begged for diversification in industry. Deploring bigotry in Welsh affairs he set the Church clearly on the path of true bi-lingualism. He pleaded against over-meticulous plans and the dating of re-union schemes saying many times how re-union had to come, but that the way to re-union was to be found by the slower path of mutual co-operation coupled with mutual understanding of each other's theological positions'.

Glyn Simon's successor as Archbishop, between 1972 and 1981, the Most Reverend Gwilym Owen Williams, Bishop of Bangor, much more personally steeped in Welsh culture than Archbishop Simon, continued his work with immense patience and skill. Archbishop Williams was widely regarded as the outstanding Christian leader in Wales, and he committed all his phenomenal intellectual powers to ensuring, in spite of some opposition, that the Church in Wales was a truly bilingual Church, ministering to *all* its children. In spite of many discouraging signs, Archbishop Williams had a sure and total trust in God's power and care. The present Bishop of St. Asaph has rightly drawn attention to Archbishop Williams's steadfast convictions, power of assimilation, ability to listen, and openness of mind. His years as Archbishop were of profound significance in the development of the Church in Wales.

(ii) Ecumenism, the Ordination of Women, and Liturgy

During the 1970s the Governing Body, which abandoned the delights of Llandrindod Wells to meet at the University College of Wales at Aberystwyth between 1975 and 1980, took important decisions on many issues, of which we might especially note Covenanting for Union with some of the Free Churches, the ordination of women as deacons, and further liturgical reform. These fields display what seems to be a distinct characteristic of the Church in Wales, an enthusiasm for new developments followed by a certain hesitation in taking matters further.

In the British ecumenical field the great interest of the 1960s lay in negotiations for union between the Anglican and Methodist Churches. At first the discussions were limited to England, but following a protest by the Church in Wales in 1963 the Church in Wales and the Methodist Church in Wales began to talk together. Opinion in Methodist circles in Wales was divided, with the Welsh-speaking congregations showing a desire to work more closely with other Free Churches in Wales while the English-speaking congregations favoured union with the Church in Wales. Within the Church in Wales the laity supported union with the Methodists much more strongly than did the clergy, although there were some areas in Wales, especially the dioceses of St. Asaph, St. Davids, and Swansea and Brecon, where the clergy were much more favourable. In the event the negotiations in England failed, and the scheme in Wales came to nothing in consequence. The debates produced some bitterness between those in favour of union and of this particular method of bringing it about and those opposed to any sort of union or to this scheme. Observers detected some hardening of attitude on the part of many members of the Church in Wales against any form of union in the later 1960s.

Since the important Faith and Order Conference of the British Council of Churches held at Nottingham in 1964 there had been considerable discussion of wider union than simply between Anglicans and Methodists. A Joint Committee to consider Covenanting for Union was established in Wales, and in September 1966 the Governing Body agreed to appoint representatives to confer further with the representatives of other churches and to report by March 1968 on the terms of a Convenant to work and pray for the inauguration of unity, on plans for practical arrangements to ensure that the act of convenanting would include members and ministers at every level, and on an agreed statement on the difference that the making of the Covenant would mean in the Churches' relationships with one another.

In 1973 the Governing Body debated the matter, and in 1974 approval was given to joining in a Covenant with the Presbyterians, the Methodists, and the new United Reformed Church. The Covenant acknowledged a common faith in Jesus Christ as Lord and Saviour, and the Churches recognized this common faith, together with their awareness of a common calling, based on a common baptism. The declaration that 'We recognize the ordained ministries of all our churches as true ministries of the word and sacraments, through which God's love is proclaimed, his grace mediated, and his Fatherly care exercised' caused much concern to some Anglicans, but on 18 January 1975 the Covenant was signed. It concluded: 'We do not yet know the form union will take. We approach our task with openness to the Spirit. We believe that God will guide his church into ways of truth and peace, correcting, strengthening, and renewing it in accordance with the mind of Christ. We therefore urge all our members to accept one another in the Holy Spirit as Jesus Christ accepts us, and to avail themselves of every opportunity to grow together through common prayer and worship in mutual understanding and love so that in every place they may be renewed together for mission. Accordingly we enter into this solemn Covenant before God and with one another, to work and pray in common obedience to our Lord Jesus Christ, in order that by the Holy Spirit we may be brought into one visible Church to serve together in mission to the glory of God the Father'.

In 1977 certain English-speaking Baptist congregations in South East Wales also signed the Covenant. But succeeding years have shown little development in working together, although in many, if not all, places there has been a more widespread feeling of good will between the different denominations, including churches not in the Covenant. The Church in Wales has, on the whole, shown little zeal for ecumenical activity. In this matter, as in so many others, an historic decision, to covenant for union, has produced few results.

For many members of the Church in Wales there is much more interest in union with the Roman Catholic Church, unrealistic as any such form of union appears during the pontificate of John Paul II. However, a Working Group on relations between the Roman Catholic Church and the Church in Wales was established in 1972, and there are regular meetings between the bishops of the two Churches. At Easter 1986 a joint Pastoral Letter from the Anglican and Roman Catholic Bishops in Wales was read in all churches of the two Communions, and just after that Easter the Most Reverend John Ward, Roman Catholic Archbishop of Cardiff, addressed the Governing Body of the Church in Wales. The Church in Wales has approved, with some reservations, the documents produced by the Anglican—Roman Catholic International Commission (A.R.C.I.C.), although it remains to be seen what difference these will make in practice.

The Orthodox Church in Wales is small, although it does include some Welsh-speaking priests, notably Archimandrite Barnabas of St. Elias Monastery, Montgomeryshire, Powys. The Church in Wales has accepted the findings of international negotiations between the Anglican Communion and the Orthodox Church, but any form of union is clearly far distant.

One obstacle to union with the Orthodox and Roman Catholic Churches is the ordination of women. The first deaconess ordained in the Church in Wales since disestablishment was set up apart for her office in 1961, and by 1969 there were three deaconesses in the Church's ministry. In the 1970s the issue of the ordination of women to the priesthood was a matter of lively debate in many Provinces of the Anglican Communion, and the Governing Body decided in April 1975 that there was no fundamental theological objection to the ordination of women to the priesthood. All the bishops were in favour, as were 87 clerical representatives and 120 lay representatives. Only 18 clerical representatives and 14 lay representatives voted against. After a short debate the Governing Body passed a motion 'that it would be inexpedient for the Church in Wales to take unilateral action in this matter at the present time'. Five years later, however, in April 1980, approval was given to the ordination of women to the diaconate, long before any other Anglican Church in the British Isles took such a step. A handful of priests left the Church in Wales in protest against the ordination of women as deacons. The Church in Wales has not subsequently taken a decision to ordain women to the priesthood. Perhaps the bishops have not wished to embarrass the Church of England, but the likelihood that the Church of Ireland will ordain women to the priesthood in 1991 may influence the Church in Wales, although such ordination of women will inevitably create tensions within the Church.

In liturgical matters the services of Baptism and Confirmation were made compulsory in 1971 after 13 years of experiment, and also in 1971 new experimental services for Candlemas, Ash Wednesday, and Holy Week were published. A Report on Christian Initiation in 1972 advocated the abolition of Confirmation, to leave Baptism as the sole rite of initiation into the Church, but in 1974 the Governing Body decided not to accept the Doctorinal Commission's recommendations. Confirmation survives in the Church in Wales. The new obligatory services of Marriage and Burial had appeared by 1975, and experimental Ordination services in 1977, by which year the hope was expressed that a new *Book of Common Prayer* for the Church in Wales could be published in 1981.

This optimistic forecast was, however, proved impossible to realise. In September 1979 the proposed new Eucharist, in connection with which 300 amendments had been debated in April 1979, failed to gain a two-thirds majority at the Governing Body. The six bishops, 65 clerical representatives, and 70 lay representatives voted for it, but 38 clerical representatives and 68 lay representatives voted against. The 1966 rite had been hailed throughout the Anglican Communion as an outstanding form of worship, but that of 1979 failed to find favour with the Governing Body. Some of its opponents found the services too conservative—

liturgical research and practice had moved on a great deal since
1966—but others, probably the majority of the lay opponents, found
it too radical. Evangelicals expressed concern about the inclusion of
prayers for the dead and about the precise nature of the Eucharistic
offering. Here again we see initial willingness to change giving way
to conservatism. Perhaps it had been a mistake to issue an
experimental rite in hard covers and to use it for 13 years.
Congregations had grown to know it well, and they liked what they
knew. Only a new rite which preserved all the essential features of
1966 had much chance of gaining the approval of the Governing
Body.

The defeat of the proposed Eucharist in 1979 delayed the
appearance of the new Prayer Book, but approval in September
1981 for what is the most conservative recent Eucharist rite in the
Anglican Communion opened the way for the publication of a *Book
of Common Prayer for use in the Church in Wales*. The first
volume, including the Eucharist and Morning and Evening Prayer,
was used in worship from 30 September 1984. The second volume,
containing Baptism, the Catechism, Confirmation, Ordination,
Marriage, the Ministry of Healing, and Burial, most of which had
already appeared in booklet form, was published in 1985. The new
book replaced the 1662 *Book of Common Prayer*, although the
services of Holy Communion (with the collects and readings from
the new Prayer Book) and Holy Matrimony in the latter could still
be used in Wales. The Preface to the new Prayer Book makes it
clear that there is to be one liturgical use in Wales, and there are
few alternatives within the services. The comparative inflexibility of
the rites is in some senses a strength and in others a weakness. The
lack of variety in the Prayer Book makes it a work which perhaps
commends itself more to those who worship once a week than to
those who worship more frequently. The 'evolved grammar' and
the many inconsistencies in the wording of the collects in English
are most unfortunate irritants.

Also in 1984 a Eucharistic rite in modern Welsh and English was
approved for experimental use. At this time it was made absolutely
clear that the *Alternative Service Book* of the Church of England was
not to be used in the Province of Wales. This was obviously a matter
of authority and not of doctrine. What is Anglican orthodoxy in
Presteigne in Powys (but in the Church of England) cannot
be heresy in Knighton in the same county (but in the Church

in Wales). Gradually the Eucharist has become the main act of worship in perhaps the majority of churches in the Province, although Morning Prayer retains a strong place in the liturgical provision of many rural churches, especially in Welsh-speaking areas. Opinion is divided on how far the *Book of Common Prayer for use in the Church in Wales* reflects a distinctively Welsh spirituality. Critics argue that it remains in essence a slightly modified version of Cranmer's English liturgy.

From 1981 an attractive Covenanting Rite in modern language has been approved for use on ecumenical occasions. Other ecumenical ventures have been less successful, especially the proposal on recognising non-episcopal ministries as outlined in a Report known as *Ministry in a Uniting Church*. The Church in Wales appears to have decided to work for the time being towards union through local ventures, rather than by any national schemes. The shared church of St. David in Pentwyn in Cardiff, the local covenant between Anglicans, Roman Catholics, and Methodists at Dinas Powys in South Glamorgan, and the formal induction of the local rector as minister of four Presbyterian churches in and around Botwnnog in North Wales point the way to future co-operation.

(iii) Finance, Structures, and Social Concern

From 1970 there was much discussion, at least in some circles, of the need for more dioceses, and a Commission was set up to explore possibilities, but no change has subsequently been made in the six existing dioceses. A radical scheme to create collegial dioceses of Llandaff and Swansea & Brecon, with the Archbishop of Wales having his cathedral at Brecon, was defeated at the Governing Body in 1980. Part of the reason for caution lay in the financial position of the Church in a time of rapid inflation. A Committee on Inflation had to be established in 1975, and the annual Quota had to be doubled from £258,000 to £516,000 in 1976. Members of the Church rose to the challenge, although in fact in 1975 the Quota contributed only 7.3% of the income of the Church, and even in 1980 only 12% came from the living members. The remainder came from endowments and investments. The decision to double stipends in real terms between 1979 and 1984 was, however, an ambitious target which was successfully attained, partly because of the continuing decline in the number of clergy.

St. David's University College, Lampeter

St. Michael's College, Llandaff

The Most Reverend D. G. Childs

The Most Reverend G. O. Williams

Archbishop Williams retired in 1982 to be succeeded by the Most Reverend Derrick Childs, Bishop of Monmouth, a noted educationalist. Although Archbishop Childs did not speak Welsh fluently, he was very well-known in Welsh society and he provided the Church in Wales with strong and determined leadership, especially in its ecumenical contacts with the Nonconformist and Roman Catholic Churches and in reforming the structures of the governance of the Church in Wales. He resigned in 1986 and in March 1987 he died as the result of a tragic road accident. His successor in the archbishopric was the Most Reverend George Noakes, Bishop of St. Davids, a pastoral and deservedly popular bishop with wide and most effective parochial experience.

A Working Party on Provincial Structures had been set up in 1980, following a Partners in Mission Consultation between 29 June and 2 July 1978, attended by three bishops from overseas, three representatives of the Covenanted Churches, and others, and after the defeat of the proposals on new dioceses. Gradually the management of the Church was reshaped during the following decade. A Board of Mission was established in 1984, to become operative in 1985, and a lay Secretary-General took up office in January 1985. The Board of Mission, headed by a full-time Director, is divided into six divisions—Communications, Ecumenism and World Mission, Education, Evangelism and Adult Education, Social Responsibility, and Stewardship. The Division for Communication is divided into three Sectors—Publications, Media Affairs, and Communication Technology. The Division for Ecumenism and World Mission is divided into two Sectors— Ecumenism and World Mission. The Division for Education is divided into three Sectors—Children's Work, Youth Work, and Statutory Education. The Division for Evangelism and Adult Education is divided into two Sectors—Evangelism and Adult Education. The Division for Social Responsibility is divided into three Sectors—The Study of Church and Society, Social Action and Liaison with Public Bodies, and International Affairs. The Division for Stewardship has no Sectors within it.

Since May 1981 the Governing Body has met at St. David's University College, Lampeter, an institution which is very familiar to many of the clergymen of the Church in Wales as the place in which they were educated. One very notable feature of the work of the Governing Body, especially since 1980, has been the consideration of reports on major social and ethical problems. For example, a report on Christians and Warfare was debated in 1981, one on World Poverty in 1982, one on Investment in South Africa in 1983, one on Rights and another on the Future of Work in Contemporary Society in 1985, one on Housing and Homelessness in 1986, and one on 'Faith in Wales' (a title adapted from the Church of England's 'Faith in the City' report) in 1988. At the meeting of the Governing Body in April 1989, the most recent meeting at the time of writing this account, discussion covered Broadcasting in the '90s, Human Fertility Services and Embryology, and Alcohol Misuse. It would be difficult to accuse the Church in the 1980s of being interested only in narrowly ecclesiastical matters, although one does wonder whether much heed is paid outside the Church to the deliberations of the Governing Body, which are often, indeed usually, of a very high standard.

(iv) Candidates for Ordination

The most worrying feature in the Church in the 1980s has undoubtedly been the continuing low number of ordinands, especially of Welsh-speaking ordinands. In 1961, when there were about 135 in training, predictions were heard that the parochial system would soon break down for lack of priests. By 1974 there were 101 in training, and in 1979 there were only 51 in training. By 1982 this number had risen to 73, but by 1989 it was only 50. Even if all these candidates are ordained there will be only about three new priests a year in each of the six dioceses in the early 1990s. In 1930 there were 969 incumbents and 376 curates in Wales, and in 1969, 748 incumbents and 182 curates, but in 1989 there were only about 526 incumbents and about 116 curates. Unless there are more candidates for ordination numbers are bound to fall yet more. A fact of immense concern lies in the statistic that of the 50 candidates in training in 1989 only five are fluent in Welsh. Since 1976, when Bishop Burgess Theological Hall at Lampeter closed, the only Theological College in Wales has been St. Michael's College at Llandaff, although some candidates have received training at St. Deiniol's Library at Hawarden in Clwyd. Many ordinands attend English theological colleges. Perhaps there were too many clergy in the Church in Wales in the past, and the lay members of the Church were not able to contribute fully to its work, but there can be no doubt that now there are too few ordinands. The parochial system survives only because of much grouping of parishes.

There has been a decline in active membership of the Church in recent years. One despondent commentator has, with considerable exaggeration, referred to the Church in Wales as a 'sect of old people'. Obviously this climate has affected vocations to the ministry. It is no longer socially necessary to belong to any church, and especially among young people the practice of any form of Christianity is unusual. Many members of the Church in Wales are members only in name. Perhaps nominal membership may be seen as a modern manifestation of medieval indulgences. One keeps one's name on the books, and perhaps occasionally contributes a pittance to the funds of the local church, on the grounds that there just might be something in religion.

Nonetheless, there are encouraging points of growth. The imaginative work of the Provincial Youth Council, the continuing enthusiasm of the Girls' Friendly Society, and the rebirth of Cymry'r Groes, the Youth Fellowship of the Church in Wales, all give grounds for hope. The creation of Rectorial Benefices and other team ministries, both urban and rural, together with the establishment of specialist ministries in hospitals, university colleges and industry, and the slow increase in the number of non-stipendiary ministers show the way to a more efficient and effective use of clergy. The absence of monks and friars, especially after the lively ministries of Mirfield fathers for several decades in Cardiff and of Franciscan friars in the 1970s and early 1980s, and also of the sisters of the Community of the Holy Name in Cardiff, is a spiritual weakness, although two religious houses of women, the Society of the Sacred Cross at Ty Mawr in Gwent and the Community of St. John the Evangelist at Bridgend in Mid Glamorgan, are powerhouses of prayer within the Church, as are the Sisters of Charity at the Retreat House at Llangasty, near Brecon. The Retreat House at Rhandirmwyn in Dyfed and the Skreen in Powys should also be mentioned.

(v) The Anglican Communion

The Church in Wales is one of the smallest provinces of the Anglican Communion in the number of its bishops, although in terms of its active membership, and certainly of its nominal membership, it is by no means the least. Attempts have been made ever since disestablishment to remind members of the Church in

Wales of the wider Anglican scene, although it was not perhaps until the appointment of bishops in Wales who had served outside Wales that a deeper, if not as yet particularly wide-spread, awareness of the Anglican Communion was apparent among people in the pews, and even in the pulpits. Bishop John Charles Jones of Bangor had served in Uganda, Bishop John Richards of St. Davids in Iran, Bishop John Poole-Hughes of Llandaff in Tanzania, and Bishop Benjamin Vaughan of Swansea and Brecon in Jamaica and Belize. Missionaries from Wales have served in many parts of the world. The Anglican Congress held at Toronto in 1963 stimulated greater interest between the various provinces of the Anglican Communion, especially through the concept of Mutual Responsibility and Interdependence, adopted in Wales in 1966. A Provincial Council for Mission and Unity was set up in 1967, and links have been established with Assam, Belize, Lesotho, Nigeria, and Tanzania. On 31 March 1970 the fiftieth anniversary of disestablishment was marked by the giving of one day's pay by members of the Church in Wales to Churches overseas. In the late 1980s there was discussion of creating a special relationship with an overseas Province within the Anglican Communion.

The Welsh bishops have attended the Lambeth Conferences from their inception, although they apparently made little impact in the years immediately after disestablishment. In more recent years, however, they have been more prominent. Archbishop Glyn Simon attended Lambeth Conferences in 1958 and 1968, coming home from the latter feeling 'very much like a kind a Rip Van Winkle returning to a world I seemed to have lost years ago'. The bishops of the Church in Wales also attend meetings of the bishops of the Church of England; possibly these discuss matters which are more familiar to them. Naturally the Church in Wales is represented at meetings of the Anglican Consultative Council—that in 1990 is to be held in Wales—and the Archbishop attends the triennial meetings of the Anglican Primates. There are also delegates from the Church in Wales at meetings of the British Council of Churches and of the World Council of Churches.

It should be noted that the Church in Wales has been in full communion since 1937 with the Old Catholic Church, since 1966 with the Philippine Independent Church, the Spanish Reformed Church and the Lusitanian Church of Portugal (the two last are now within the Anglican Communion), and since 1975 with the

Mar Thoma Syrian Church, and it is also in communion with the Churches of South India, North India, Pakistan, and Bangladesh, churches made up of several former denominations, including the Anglican Church, in those countries.

6

Conclusion

What of the Church in Wales seventy years after disestablishment? Has it taken full advantage of its unsought freedom? Does it still retain too many vestiges of its old privileged state? Is it isolated in Wales? Is it marginal to Welsh society?

The Church in Wales has the strengths and weaknesses of a relatively small Church. It remains the largest denomination in Wales, although in terms of regular worshippers it is only slightly larger than the Roman Catholic Church. It is, however, more in evidence in Welsh society than is the Roman Catholic Church. Nonconformist denominations have declined considerably in membership since 1920, and it has rightly been said that many Nonconformists probably look back with nostalgia to their golden years before disestablishment. The Church in Wales appears to be conservative in its attitudes, especially in ecumenism and in liturgy, sometimes 'like a mighty tortoise' slow to act.

The dioceses in Wales are large in population by standards of the Anglican Communion as a whole, and the bishops are required to undertake an almost impossible range of duties, ever increasing if we compare them with earlier years. In particular the work expected of the Archbishop is quite excessive, with many Provincial commitments over and above the care of a diocese. It may soon be time to detach the office of Archbishop from that of oversight of one of the existing diocese, although he surely should have a small diocese in which to exercise his pastoral ministry. But the Archbishop should be free to preach and teach throughout Wales to strengthen both his own Church and other Christian denominations.

The procedures of the Governing Body are rather cumbersome,

and there is considerable recognition of this. Before disestablishment Bishop Owen of St. Davids expressed great apprehension about the ability of the Church in Wales to run its own affairs: 'What I dread most is the dreadful apparition of a Welsh synod, messing about with the big, complex, and far reaching questions which now perplex all the combined wisdom of the Church of England'. He felt that such a synod might be too easily swayed by 'tribal jealousies' and 'nationalistic vanities'. A study of the work of the Governing Body soon shows that Bishop Owen's worries were on the whole not justified, although on some issues, possibly above all on liturgical revision, the Church in Wales has insisted on doing work largely on its own, when it might have been better to have collaborated much more closely with the Church of England, perhaps to the extent of using the same books in some cases. The Church in Wales is not quite unique in responding to any new problem by setting up a new committee or sub-committee.

Some members of the Church in Wales doubtless wish that their Church was still established. They long to be in a Church of which the Queen is Governor, and they would like to see their bishops in the House of Lords. It is perhaps a small sign of regret at being disestablished that a Welsh bishop is today probably addressed, at least in some rural dioceses, as 'My Lord' more often than is his episcopal brother in the established Church of England, although the 'lordship' of a Bishop does not, of course, derive from membership of the Upper House.

Financially the Church has survived disestablishment, although it might be argued that too much money is spent in maintaining the status quo ('keeping the show on the road'). Too few clergy minister in too many church, often in very large groups; a leaner and fitter Church, with fewer churches, might be in a better position to proclaim the Gospel to contemporary Wales. Certainly more clergy are needed, but if they emerge they will have to be paid for, although the financial demands on members do not as yet add up to much more than small change as far as most individuals are concerned. The ministry of the laity has not yet been taken seriously in many parishes, and most lay people have not yet learnt how to give their time, talents, and money to the Church. Mention should, however, be made here of the invaluable contribution to the Church's work made by readers, formerly known as lay readers, men and women who are licensed to assist the clergy in liturgical and pastoral ministry.

In recent years there has been some growth of parties within the Church. The Anglo-Catholic Church Union is strong in some parts of Wales, and the Evangelical Fellowship of the Church in Wales is growing in numbers and influence. The Charismatic Movement has brought new life to many parishes, although it is not without attendant dangers. Nonetheless, all, or almost all, those who are adherents of these parties are also firmly rooted within the Anglican tradition. Differences of viewpoints can produce creative tension within the Body of Christ.

The Church in Wales still retains its integrity. It seeks to serve the whole of Wales and all the people who live here. It ministers to those who are naturally and unselfconsciously Welsh in speech, to those, often learners, who are zealous for the Welsh language, to those who regret that they cannot speak Welsh, to those who are unconcerned about Welsh, to those who are hostile to Welsh, and to those who have come to live in Wales. It preaches the Gospel in North Wales, Mid Wales, West Wales, and South Wales. It cannot any longer be regarded as 'yr hen estrones' ['the old stranger'] or as the Church of England in Wales.

Mr. Gladstone predicted, with regard to disestablishment, that death would be followed by resurrection. The Church in Wales died as an established church; to what extent has it risen to new life?

This essay has said much about archbishops, bishops, and the Governing Body, and they have their part to play in the work of the Church. But I am sure that what really matters is the parish. Disestablishment did not, could not, destroy the parochial system of the Church in Wales. In city, town, valley, village, and hamlet the life and work of over 1,000 parish churches is the essential work of the Church. Words used by Canon Roger Lloyd in his magisterial *The Church of England 1900-1975* are also true of Wales: 'The real history of the Church of England is therefore mostly made in its parish churches, and the parish priest is the pivot on which that history turns. The Church might possibly survive a whole generation of impossible bishops and dead cathedrals. . .But it could not possibly survive a whole generation of bad vicars and lethargic parish churches. For the parish church is the centre of the Church's life, and "the main stream of Anglican piety flows, as it has always flowed, through the parish churches: and therefore it is the parishes that are the exciting thing. The life of the parish is Church

History'''. The parishes are, in a favourite phrase of Archbishop Noakes, 'in the front line'.

And the parishes are made up of the faithful and not so faithful. To adapt some words of Bishop Mervyn Stockwood of Southwark: 'Whether or not the Lord strides triumphantly through Wales or stumbles as a paralytic will be determined not by the Archbishop of Wales but by us who are his limbs'. Or as Dom Gregory Dix remarked: 'The most moving of the reflections which Christians history brings is not the thought of great events or of well remembered Christian saints but, instead, that of the countless host of faithful Christians who leave no memorial in the pages of history'.

The work of the Church is to nurture personal awareness of Jesus Christ in each of its members. When people make the request 'we wish to see Jesus' (John, 12, v. 21), the Church must present its Lord to them, so that the individual comes to know his or her Saviour. From that knowledge will come the desire to worship in the fellowship of the Church and the desire to serve the community. It is on its efforts to bring about that commitment that the whole work of the Church must be judged. It must be centred on God. It must be open to God. It must listen to God. It must live in the freedom of the Gospel.

There are abundant signs that God's blessing still rests upon his Church in Wales under the energetic and pastoral leadership of Archbishop George Noakes and his brethren on the Bench of Bishops. The Church is entering the 1990s, the world-wide Anglican Decade of Evangelism, in good heart.

One may perhaps conclude by recalling again some words of Lord Sankey in 1922: 'Give me leave in my last words to recall that the Church in Wales is the Church of Christ. Let us listen for the faintest whisper of His voice. To know what He wishes and to obey what He commands is the one sure salvation for our country and ourselves'.

APPENDIX I

The Organization of the Church in Wales

(i) The Province

The Province of Wales covers almost the whole of Wales and is headed by the Archbishop of Wales, who is also Bishop of one of the six dioceses. The Archbishop is elected by the Archbishop's Electoral College, made up of the diocesan bishops and elected clerical and lay members from every diocese. If the Electoral College is not held within three months of the earliest day on which it can be held, or if, having been assembled, it is unable to elect, which requires a two-thirds majority, within three days, the Archbishop of Canterbury is to appoint the new Archbishop. (It has never been necessary to employ this procedure.)

The Governing Body of the Church in Wales, made up of bishops, deans, archdeacons, and *ex-officio*, elected, and co-opted clerical and lay members, legislates for the Church. The Archbishop is President of the Governing Body. The six diocesan bishops represent the 'ancient Provincial Synod'. The Governing Body sits in three Orders, those of bishops, clergy, and laity, and it must meet at least once a year. It usually meets twice a year at Eastertide and in September, since 1981 at St. David's University College, Lampeter. The Standing Committee of the Governing Body, which must meet at least three times a year, plays an increasingly important part in the work of the Church. Its role is to advise the Governing Body on policy, especially on long-term planning and on priorities in the use of resources. Sub-committees of the Standing Committee include the Drafting Committee, the Business Committee, the Appointments Committee, and the Legal Committee.

The Representative Body, also made up of bishops and of elected, co-opted, and nominated clerical and lay members, cares for the

The Bishops in 1990
Swansea and Brecon — Assistant St. Davids — Monmouth — Llandaff
St. Asaph — St. Davids (Archbishop) — Bangor

Sir William Gladstone
(Chairman of the Representative Body)

Mr. David McIntyre
(Secretary-General)

property of the Church. Its Finance and Resources Committee has a key role in carrying out the Representative Body's executive functions. Sub-committees of the Finance and Resources Committee include the Investment Committee, the Staff and Services Committee, the Property Committee, the Maintenance of Ministry Committee, and the Bishops' Residences and Expenses Committee. The Covenants Department is under the control of the Representative Body.

A lay Secretary-General oversees the work of the Board of Mission, the Governing Body, the Archbishop's Registry, and the Representative Body.

The Provincial Board of Mission, headed by a full-time Director, is divided into six Divisions—Communications, Ecumenism and World Mission, Education, Evangelism and Adult Education, Social Responsibility, and Stewardship. The Division for Communication is divided into three Sectors—Publications, Media Affairs, and Communication Technology. The Division for Ecumenism and World Mission is divided into two Sectors— Ecumenism and World Mission. The Division for Education is divided into three Sectors—Children's Work, Youth Work, and Statutory Education. The Division for Evangelism and Adult Education is divided into two Sectors—Evangelism and Adult Education. The Division for Social Responsibility is divided into three Sectors—The Study of Church and Society, Social Action and Liaison with Public Bodies, and International Affairs. The Division for Stewardship has no Sectors within it.

The Ministry Committee of the Bench of Bishops (incorporating the work of the former Central Committee for the Training or Ordinands and the Provincial Selection Board) is responsible for the selection and training of candidates for the ministry. Three sub-committees of the Ministry Committee cover Nurture and Selection for the Ordained Ministry, Resources for Training, and the Evaluation of Theological Education for the Ordained Ministry.

Other important bodies responsible to the Bench of Bishops are the Doctrinal Commission and the Standing Liturgical Advisory Group.

The Provincial Board of Patronage is made up of the diocesan bishops, the Chairman of the Representative Body or his or her nominee, and an elected lay person representing the diocese in which the vacant parish is situated. It appoints an incumbent to a benefice on every third vacancy in a rotation of four.

The Archbishop may hold a Visitation of his Province if he so wishes.

The Provincial Court, with four ecclesiastical and six lay judges, is normally a final court for clerical and lay members of the Church in Wales to settle contentious issues. The Special Provincial Court, made up of the Archbishop, the remaining diocesan bishops, and the judges of the Provincial Court, hears any case against any of the bishops, diocesan and assistant. The Supreme Court, made up of the Archbishops of Canterbury, York, Armagh, and Dublin, and the Primus of the Scottish Episcopal Church, sitting with four assessors, hears any case against the Archbishop, together with certain appeals.

(ii) The Diocese

The diocese is usually regarded as the fundamental unit, 'the local church', the Province being a voluntary association of dioceses. Each diocese is governed by a bishop, elected by an Electoral College, made up of the diocesan bishops and elected clerical and lay members from every diocese. As with the Archbishop's Electoral College, if the Electoral College is not held within three months of the earliest day on which it can be held, or if, having been assembled, it is unable to elect with three days, the Archbishop of Canterbury is to appoint the new bishop. (This procedure has never had to be employed either.) The election of a diocesan bishop must be confirmed by the diocesan bishops sitting as the Sacred Synod. The diocesan bishop may have the help of an assistant bishop, nominated by him and approved by the other diocesan bishops.

Every diocese has a cathedral, which is under the jurisdiction of the dean and chapter. The chapter is made up of archdeacons and canons or prebendaries. These are usually senior clerics within the diocese, and they are normally also incumbents of parishes within the diocese. The bishop has his throne or chair in the cathedral, which is the Mother Church of the diocese.

The Diocesan Conference is made up of elected, *ex-officio*, nominated, and co-opted members, clerical and lay. It must meet at least once a year.

A diocese also has many committees, including the Diocesan Board of Finance, the Standing Committee, the Diocesan Ministry Committee, the Diocesan Parsonage Board, the Diocesan Council for Education, the Diocesan Council for Social Responsibility, the Diocesan Council for Mission and Unity, the Diocesan Stewardship Committee, the Diocesan Board of Patronage, the Diocesan Churches Committee, which deals with redundant churches, and the Diocesan Advisory Committee, which considers the artistic quality of gifts, such as stained-glass windows, memorial tablets, and furnishings, to churches.

The Diocesan Board of Patronage, which includes two representatives from the vacant parish, appoints an incumbent to a benefice on every second and fourth turn in a rotation of four. The bishop alone appoints an incumbent to a benefice on every first vacancy in a rotation of four.

The bishop may hold a Visitation of his diocese or of part of his diocese as he wishes.

Each diocese has a Diocesan Court, presided over by the chancellor of the diocese, a judge. He should not be confused with the chancellor of the cathedral, who is a cleric.

(iii) The Archdeaconry

An archdeacon has responsibility under the diocesan bishop for the parishes in his archdeaconry. The dioceses of St. Asaph and St. Davids each contain three archdeaconries; the remaining four dioceses contain two each. The archdeacon makes a Visitation of the parishes within his archdeaconry at regular intervals; from time to time the archdeacon's visitational jurisdiction is suspended when the bishop carries out his Visitation. The archdeacon may hold an Archdeacon's Court. The archdeacon may be a 'full-time' archdeacon, or he may hold his office together with a parochial appointment.

(iv) The Rural Deanery

A rural dean has responsibility under the diocesan bishop and the archdeacon for the parishes in his or her rural deanery, a number of parishes, often centred on the local town. The office of rural dean is not a full-time appointment; he or she serves also as a parish cleric within the rural deanery. When a benefice is vacant the rural dean has the care of that parish.

The Ruridecanal Conference, made up of the clergy working within the rural deanery and of elected representatives from the parishes, together with coopted members, meets from time to time to consider matters of common interest. Some Ruridecanal Conferences meet frequently, while others meet only once a year, although by the Constitution of the Church in Wales Ruridecanal Conferences should meet at least four times a year.

The clerics of a rural deanery meet together from time to time, often monthly, in the Ruridecanal Chapter, to discuss subjects of mutual concern and for study.

(v) The Parish

At parochial level an incumbent (rector or vicar) may be assisted by one or more assistant curates. In a Rectorial Benefice the clerical staff consists of a rector, one or more vicars, and normally one or more curates. An incumbent may be incumbent of one parish or of several grouped parishes. Each parish within a group has a parish church, and there may also be daughter or mission churches.

In every parish there is an electoral roll on which lay communicants over the age of 16 years may have their names entered as qualified electors. An Annual Vestry Meeting must be held every year before 30 April in every parish. Other Vestry Meetings may be held at other times. The Annual Vestry Meeting discusses the mission of the Church in the parish: pastoral, evangelistic, social, and ecumenical. The Annual Vestry Meeting also elects one of the churchwardens, the other being appointed by the incumbent, and the Parochial Church Council, together with sidesmen and parochial representatives on ruridecanal and diocesan bodies.

Almost all parishes have two churchwardens, although some may by custom have more. The churchwardens are required by the Constitution to represent the laity in the parish, to 'promote peace and unity amongst parishioners, and by example and precept to encourage the parishioners in the practice of true religion'. They are also to maintain order and decency in the church and churchyard. Churchwardens may not serve for more than six consecutive years, except with permission from the archdeacon.

The Parochial Church Council, made up usually of the clergy serving in the parish, the churchwardens, and lay members over 18 years of age, elected by the Annual Vestry Meeting, should meet at least four times in every year. It is to consult and co-operate with the incumbent 'in all matters of concern and importance to the parish'. The Parochial Church Council appoints a secretary and treasurer. Many parishes have a Standing Committee and also sub-committees for specific areas of parochial life.

Appendix II

The Archbishops of Wales

1920.   Alfred George Edwards, Bishop of St. Asaph.
      Enthroned Archbishop 1 June 1920.
      Resigned as Archbishop and Bishop 25 July 1934.

1934.   Charles Alfred Howell Green, Bishop of Bangor.
      Enthroned Archbishop 18 December 1934.
      Resigned as Archbishop 12 April 1944.

1944.   David Lewis Prosser, Bishop of St. Davids
      Enthroned Archbishop 7 November 1944.
      Resigned as Archbishop 30 April 1949.

1949.   John Morgan, Bishop of Llandaff.
      Enthroned Archbishop 21 September 1949.
      Died 26 June 1957.

1957.   Alfred Edwin Morris, Bishop of Monmouth.
      Enthroned Archbishop 19 December 1957.
      Resigned as Archbishop and Bishop 31 December
      1967;

1968.   William Glyn Hughes Simon, Bishop of Llandaff.
      Enthroned Archbishop 17 July 1968.
      Resigned as Archbishop 30 June 1971.

1971.   Gwilym Owen Williams, Bishop of Bangor.
      Enthroned Archbishop 21 September 1971.
      Resigned as Archbishop and Bishop 30 September
      1982.

1983.   Derrick Greenslade Childs, Bishop of Monmouth.
      Enthroned Archbishop 15 March 1983.
      Resigned as Archbishop and Bishop 30 June 1986.

1987.   George Noakes, Bishop of St. Davids.
      Enthroned Archbishop 14 January 1987.

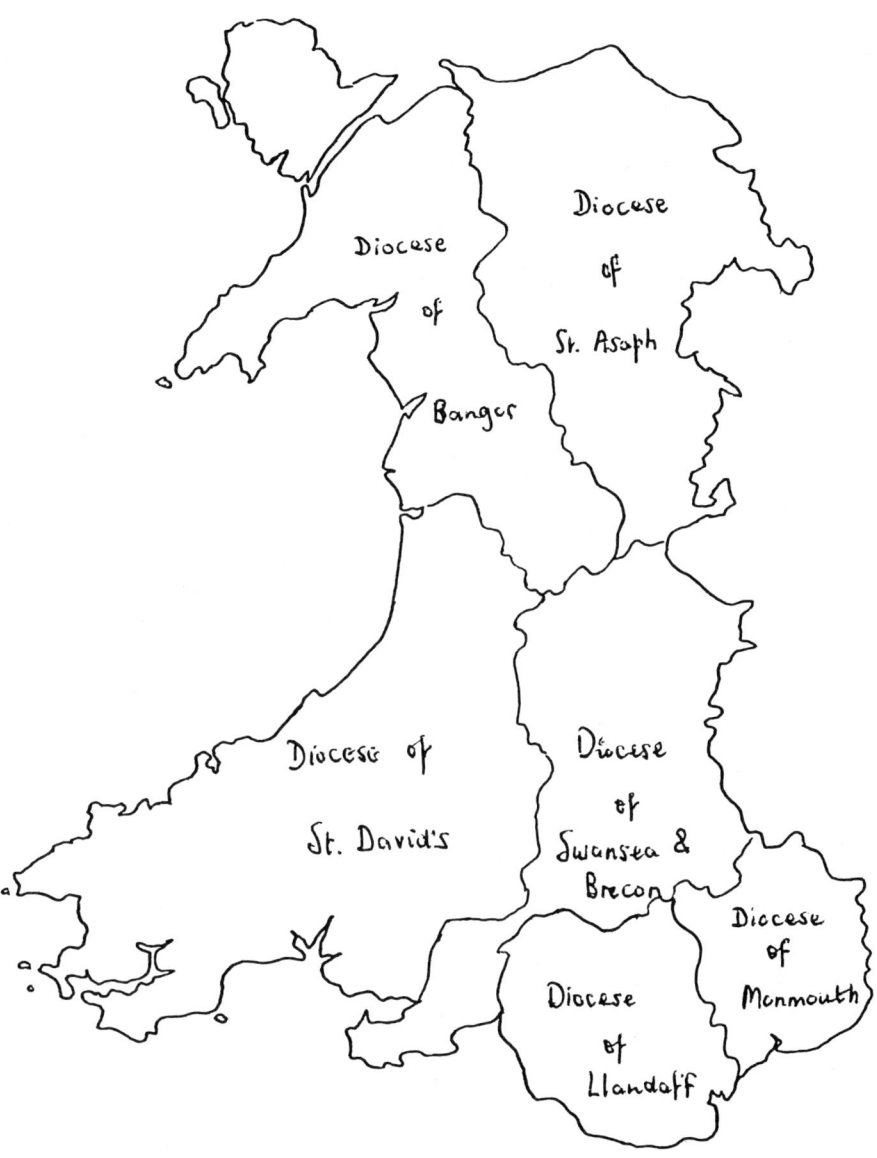

A Map of the Dioceses of the Church in Wales

Appendix III

The Dioceses of Wales

(A) St. Asaph

The Diocese of St. Asaph (1,025,256 acres) was made up of virtually the whole of Denbighshire and almost the whole of Flintshire, together with a sizeable part of Montgomeryshire, a considerable part of Merionethshire, a small part of Caernarfonshire, and a tiny part of Shropshire; since local government reorganization in April 1974 it has covered almost the whole of Clwyd and a considerable part of Powys around Newtown and Welshpool, together with some parishes in Gwynedd around Bala and Llanrwst and a tiny part of Shropshire. The total population in 1981 was about 430,000; Easter Communicants in 1988 were 22,301.

It is divided into three Archdeaconries. The Archdeaconry of St. Asaph includes the Rural Deaneries of St. Asaph, Denbigh, Dyffryn Clwyd, Holywell, Llanrwst, and Rhos, the Archdeaconry of Montgomery includes the Rural Deaneries of Cedewain, Caereinion, Llanfyllin, and Pool, and the Archdeaconry of Wrexham includes the Rural Deaneries of Bangor Isycoed, Edeyrnion, Llangollen, Mold, Penllyn, and Wrexham.

The heart of the Diocese is the small city of St. Asaph in the beautiful Vale of Clwyd, a few miles from Rhyl on the North Wales coast. The Cathedral is one of the smallest ancient cathedrals in England and Wales, although its fine proportions give it the appearance of being larger than it is. Outside the Cathedral stands the monument to the translators of the Bible into Welsh.

The Diocese extends over a wide area, including many different regions. The North Wales coast provides ample opportunities for ministry to holiday makers and also to many retired people. Deeside and Wrexham, which is the largest town in North Wales and the see of a Roman Catholic Bishop, are areas of economic and population growth, looking as much to Chester and Liverpool as to Wales. The Vale of Clwyd and areas to the south of it as far as Newtown in Powys have more scattered populations and are primarily agricultural, although Newtown itself has an increasing population. While there is a relatively strong sense of identity in the Clwyd part of the Diocese, the Archdeaconry of Montgomery seems to be very distant from the rest of the Diocese, and its natural links are far more with Shrewsbury.

St. Deiniol's Library, Hawarden, a residential institution, has a long tradition of training candidates for the ministry, for neighbouring English dioceses as well as for Welsh dioceses.

Although this Diocese is not as Welsh in speech as its western neighbour, Bangor, there are large areas, especially around Bala and Llanrwst, in the Denbighshire uplands, and in parts of Montgomeryshire, in which Welsh is still the dominant language, and Welsh services are held in many of the towns and villages elsewhere in the Diocese. In common with other Welsh-speaking regions in Wales the Diocese is experiencing increasing difficulty in finding priests and deacons who can minister in Welsh, although many clerics who have learned Welsh work with considerable success in many parishes.

Bishops of St. Asaph since Disestablishment

1889.   Alfred George Edwards. Consecrated 25 March 1889.
        Also Archbishop of Wales. Enthroned Archbishop
        1 June 1920.
        Resigned as Archbishop and Bishop 25 July 1934.
1934.   William Thomas Havard. Consecrated 29 September
        1934.
        Translated to St. Davids 1950.
1950.   David Daniel Bartlett. Consecrated 21 September 1950.
        Resigned 31 December 1970.
1971.   Harold John Charles. Consecrated 25 March 1971.
        Resigned 31 March 1982.
1982.   Alwyn Rice Jones. Consecrated 29 June 1982.

Suffragan Bishop of Maenan

1928.   Thomas Lloyd. Consecrated 30 November 1928.
        Died 15 March 1935.

(B) Bangor

The Diocese of Bangor (985,946 acres) was made up of the county of Anglesey, together with almost the whole of Caernarfonshire, the greater part of Merionethshire, and the western part of Montgomeryshire; since local government reorganization in April 1974 it has covered almost the whole of Gwynedd, together with a portion of Powys around Machynlleth and Llanidloes. The total population in 1981 was about 225,000; Easter Communicants in 1988 were 12,948.

It is divided into two Archdeaconries. The Archdeaconry of Bangor includes the Rural Deaneries of Arfon, Arllechwedd, Llifon and Talybolion, Menai and Malldraeth, Tindaethwy, and Twrcelyn, and the Archdeaconry of Merioneth includes the Rural Deaneries of Ardudwy, Arwystli, Cyfeiliog and Mawddwy, Eifionydd, Llŷn, and Ystumaner. It is the only diocese to have preserved the names of the ancient territorial units for all its rural deaneries.

The unpretentious but attractive Cathedral of St. Deiniol is said to be on the oldest cathedral site in Britain with an uninterrupted history. It has recently become part of a Rectorial Benefice covering the lively City of Bangor, which is the home of the University College of North Wales.

From its centre in the heartland of Gwynedd, close to Island of Anglesey and to the mountains of Snowdonia, the Diocese stretches down to the south for 100 miles, beyond the town of Llanidloes in Powys to the parish of Llangurig on the borders of Radnorshire.

Economically the Diocese is for the most part poor in the quality of its land and it has little heavy industry. The decline of slate quarrying has created many problems in Blaenau Ffestiniog and around Snowdonia. Holyhead is a major port for travel to Ireland. Unemployment, especially seasonal unemployment, is high in many parts of the Diocese. Tourism is a major and growing industry in what is one of the most scenically beautiful areas of Britain, with its mountains, sea coasts, and castles, but the existence of hundreds of 'second homes' presents a serious challenge to the survival of indigenous local communities. There are few large towns, and the population of many rural areas has declined. Although the population of the coastal areas has increased, this has largely been as the result of immigration from England, and Welsh is endangered in many villages.

Gwynedd remains, however, the most Welsh-speaking county in Wales, and the shortage of Welsh-speaking priests has been felt strongly here. The total number of clergymen in the Diocese has halved during the past 30 years, and parishes have been grouped together in units which may comprise seven or eight churches. There are undoubtedly too many churches in parts of the Diocese, especially in Anglesey and Llŷn, and many have actually been closed. Some priests have learned Welsh and they serve in an increasing number of parishes, but it is difficult to see how there can be a really effective pastoral ministry in this Diocese until more native speakers of Welsh come forward for ordination.

Bishops of Bangor since Disestablishment

1899. Watkin Herbert Williams. Consecrated 2 February 1899.
        Resigned 31 December 1924.
1925. Daniel Davies, Consecrated 24 February 1925.
        Died 23 August 1928.
1928. Charles Alfred Howell Green.
        Translated from Monmouth 1928.
        Also Archbishop of Wales. Enthroned Archbishop 18 December 1934.
        Resigned as Archbishop 12 April 1944.
        Died 7 May 1944.
1944. David Edwardes Davies. Consecrated 25 July 1944.
        Resigned 1 November 1948.
1949. John Charles Jones. Consecrated 6 January 1949.
        Died 13 October 1956.
1957. Gwilym Owen Williams. Consecrated 1 May 1957.
        Also Archbishop of Wales. Enthroned Archbishop 21 September 1971.
        Resigned as Archbishop and Bishop 30 September 1982.
1982. John Cledan Mears. Consecrated 21 December 1982.

(C) St. Davids

The Diocese of St. Davids (1,416,563 acres) covered, after the creation of the Diocese of Swansea and Brecon in 1923, the former counties of Cardiganshire, Carmarthenshire, and Pembrokeshire, together with a very small part of Glamorgan; since local government reorganization in April 1974 it has been virtually coterminous with the County of Dyfed. The total population in 1981 was about 330,000; Easter Communicants in 1988 were 23,273.

It is divided into three Archdeaconries. The Archdeaconry of St. Davids includes the Rural Deaneries of Castlemartin, Daugleddau, Dewisland and Fishguard, Narberth, and Roose, the Archdeaconry of Cardigan includes the Rural Deaneries of Cemais and Sub-Aeron, Emlyn, Glyn Aeron, Lampeter and Ultra-Aeron, and Llanbadarn Fawr, and the Archdeaconry of Carmarthen includes the Rural Deaneries of Carmarthen, Dyffryn Aman, Kidwelly, Llangadog and Llandeilo, and St. Clears.

The Cathedral of St. David and St. Andrew is one of the outstanding buildings in Wales. It lies in the small village-city of St. Davids, on the far west of the peninsula of Dewisland, where, in Francis Kilvert's words, 'the patron saint of Wales sleeps by the western sea'. The Cathedral is also a parish church.

The Diocese remains the largest in area in Wales even after its division in 1923, and poor communications make it difficult to develop a strong sense of diocesan or county identity. Loyalties are still largely to the former constituent counties, especially in Pembrokeshire. The Bishop lives in Abergwili, just outside Carmarthen, very much in the centre of the Diocese, and almost 50 miles from his Cathedral. At present the Bishop of St. Davids is also Archbishop of Wales, and to assist him in his numerous commitments there is an Assistant Bishop, who is also Archdeacon of St. Davids.

Parts of the Diocese have high unemployment, although other areas are economically very prosperous in both agriculture and industry. Fishguard is a major port for Ireland. Tourism is important in the local economy especially in the Pembrokeshire National Park and along the coast of Cardiganshire.

Much of the Diocese is rural and bilingual, although South Pembrokeshire has for centuries been 'little England beyond Wales', where the Welsh language is seldom heard. The south eastern part of Carmarthenshire, especially around the large town of Llanelli, appears at present to be losing its Welsh, especially among its younger people, although the language survives more strongly around Ammanford. The immigration of English families is transforming the cultural life of many towns and villages in the Diocese.

St. David's University College at Lampeter was for over a century the main seminary for training priests in Wales; now it is a constituent college of the federal University of Wales, as is the University College of Wales at Aberystwyth, one of the larger towns in the Diocese.

In this Diocese, too, there is a crisis in the supply of Welsh-speaking priests, although here also many priests have learned the language and minister even in the heartland.

Bishops of St. Davids since Disestablishment

1897. John Owen. Consecrated 1 May 1897.
       Died 4 November 1926.
1927. David Lewis Prosser. Consecrated 2 February 1927.
       Also Archbishop of Wales. Enthroned Archbishop
       7 November 1944.
       Resigned as Archbishop 30 April 1949.
       Died 28 February 1950.
1950. William Thomas Havard. Translated from St. Asaph
       1950.
       Died 17 August 1956.
1956. John Richards Richards. Consecrated 6 December 1956.
       Resigned 3 March 1971.
1971. Eric Matthias Roberts. Consecrated 1 June 1971.
       Resigned 30 September 1981.
1982. George Noakes. Consecrated 2 February 1982.
       Also Archbishop of Wales. Enthroned Archbishop 14
       January 1987

Suffragan and Assistant Bishops since Disestablishment

1915. Edward Latham Bevan.
       Consecrated Suffragan Bishop of Swansea 29
       September 1915.
       Translated to Swansea and Brecon 1923.
1988. John Ivor Rees.
       Consecrated Assistant Bishop of St. Davids 25 April
       1988.

(D) Llandaff

The Diocese of Llandaff (518,863 acres) covered, after the creation of the Diocese of Monmouth in 1921, part of the former county of Glamorgan; since local government reorganization in April 1974 it has included almost the whole of Mid Glamorgan and most of South Glamorgan, together with half of West Glamorgan. The total population in 1981 was about 980,000; Easter Communicants in 1988 were 27,388.

It is divided into two Archdeaconries. The Archdeaconry of Llandaff includes the Rural Deaneries of Bridgend, Caerphilly, Llantwit Major and Cowbridge, Llandaff, and Penarth and Barry, and the Archdeaconry of Margam includes the Rural Deaneries of Aberdare, Margam, Merthyr Tydfil, Neath, Pontypridd, and Rhondda.

The Cathedral of SS. Peter and Paul with SS. Dyfrig, Teilo, and Euddogwy, which is also a parish church, is situated in the suburb of Llandaff in the City of Cardiff, capital of Wales since 1955 and also the see of a Roman Catholic Archbishop. The Cathedral was very seriously damaged by a landmine on 2 January 1941. It was subsequently restored under the direction of Mr. George Pace. Its interior is dominated by Sir Jacob Epstein's 'Majestas'. This is the only Cathedral in Wales to have a Choir School.

The Diocese is the most densely populated and industrialized in Wales. Half the population of Wales lives within 25 miles of Cardiff. Some parishes in Cardiff have larger populations than those of entire archdeaconries in the rest of Wales. The area of the Diocese is relatively compact; with recently improved roads few parishes are more than 45 minutes travel from the Bishop's house.

Although much of the Diocese is urban and industrial, notably Cardiff and the valleys, it also includes many very attractive rural parishes, especially in the Vale of Glamorgan. Glamorgan, a larger area than this Diocese, is home to one quarter of the Welsh speakers in Wales, but they form a relatively small proportion of the total population. Social and economic changes have produced many problems and tensions in Glamorgan, the decline of traditional industries having produced high unemployment in some parts of the Diocese, which has a long tradition of seeking to present the 'Social Gospel' in action. The tragedy of Aberfan occurred in this Diocese on 21 October 1966. The ecumenical

Glamorgan Industrial Mission has existed since 1974, developing work in industrial chaplaincy initiated by the Diocese of Llandaff. The parish of Penydarren, near Merthyr Tydfil, with its Urban Theology Unit and its imaginative Dan-y-Castell Farm project, deserved special mention.

Most Christian denominations and sects are to be found in Cardiff, which also presents the challenge of other faiths.

St. Michael's College at Llandaff is the only Theological College in the Province of Wales. The University of Wales College of Cardiff is by far the largest constituent institution of the University of Wales, and within the Diocese there are also the University College of Medicine in Cardiff and the Polytechnic of Wales at Pontypridd.

Bishops of Llandaff since Disestablishment

1905. Joshua Pritchard Hughes. Consecrated 1 June 1905.
        Resigned 1931.
1931. Timothy Rees. Consecrated 25 April 1931.
        Died 29 April 1939.
1939. John Morgan. Translated from Swansea and Brecon
        1939.
        Also Archbishop of Wales. Enthroned Archbishop
        21 September 1949.
        Died 26 June 1957.
1957. William Glyn Hughes Simon. Translated from Swansea
        and Brecon 1957.
        Also Archbishop of Wales. Enthroned Archbishop
        17 July 1968.
        Resigned as Archbishop 30 June 1971.
        Resigned as Bishop 31 August 1971.
1971. Eryl Stephen Thomas. Translated from Monmouth
        1971.
        Resigned 5 November 1975.
1975. John Richard Worthington Poole-Hughes.
        Consecrated Bishop of South West Tanganyika
        31 May 1962. Bishop of Llandaff 1975.
        Resigned 31 July 1985.
1985. Roy Thomas Davies. Consecrated 1 November 1985.

Assistant Bishop in the Province of Wales
(Resident in the Diocese of Llandaff)

1946. Richard William Jones. Consecrated 29 June 1946.
Died 2 June 1953.

Bishops Consecrated as Assistant Bishops of Llandaff

1961. Thomas Maurice Hughes. Consecrated 29 June 1961.
Resigned 1977.
1977. David Reece. Consecrated 29 September 1977.
Resigned 1983.

(E) Monmouth

The Diocese of Monmouth (342,854 acres) was virtually coterminous with the former County of Monmouthshire; since local government reorganization in April 1974 is has covered almost the whole of Gwent, together with some parts of Mid Glamorgan and South Glamorgan. The total population in 1981 was about 520,000; Easter Communicants in 1988 were 13,691.

It is divided into two Archdeaconries. The Archdeaconry of Monmouth includes the Rural Deaneries of Abergavenny, Chepstow, Monmouth, Netherwent, and Raglan and Usk, and the Archdeaconry of Newport includes the Rural Deaneries of Bassaleg, Bedwellty, Blaenau Gwent, Newport, and Pontypool.

The Diocese was created out of the ancient Diocese of Llandaff, and it came into being on 18 October 1921. The first Bishop was the Right Reverend Charles Alfred Howell Green, formerly Archdeacon of Monmouth. The parish church of St. Woolos in Newport became the Pro-Cathedral of the Diocese in 1921, and a Chapter was formed in 1930. In 1949 St. Woolos's was formally made the Cathedral, and in the early 1960s it was considerably extended by the addition of a new quire and sanctuary to the design of Mr. Adrian Caroe. It remains the parish church of a large parish.

Monmouth is the smallest diocese in area in the Church in Wales, few parishes being more than twenty miles from Newport.

The eastern part of the diocese is very rural, with a large number of small and ancient churches, while the western half contains many industrial and urban parishes, including the eastern part of the City of Cardiff. The new town of Cwmbran has offered a massive challenge to the Diocese.

Words written in 1971 by Canon E. T. Davies, the doyen of Church historians in Wales, still remain true: 'The diocese of Monmouth is virtually coterminous with the county of Monmouth, and the key to the history of the latter is its geographical position as a border county. This factor has influenced the county profoundly: the eastern parishes merge into Herefordshire and Gloucestershire; the south east has felt the pull of the Severn crossing and Bristol for centuries; the parishes along the Rhymney river look to Glamorgan rather than to Monmouthshire, and populous parishes like Rumney, Cyncoed, and Llanedeyrn are in the City of Cardiff. The population is probably more mixed than in any other county in Wales, and the Welsh language has nearly died out, even in Nonconformist circles. New industrial belts have come into existence since 1945, inevitably accompanied by very large new housing estates. This is an industrial expansion which is likely to continue, and people are beginning to wonder how much of the Caldicot moors and the so-called Wentloog moors (i.e. the riparian country between Chepstow and Cardiff) will be left by the end of this century. Soon the county will be known as Gwent, and the change of name will make no difference: it is unlikely to "settle down" for a long time to come'.

Bishops of Monmouth

1921. Charles Alfred Howell Green.
       Consecrated 21 December 1921.
       Translated to Bangor, 1928.
1928. Gilbert Cunningham Joyce.
       Consecrated 30 November 1928.
       Resigned 30 April 1940.
1940. Alfred Edwin Monahan. Consecrated 24 August 1940.
       Died 10 August 1945.
1945. Alfred Edwin Morris. Consecrated 1 November 1945.
       Also Archbishop of Wales. Enthroned Archbishop 19 December 1957.
       Resigned as Archbishop and Bishop 31 December 1967.

1968. Eryl Stephen Thomas. Consecrated 29 March 1968.
Translated to Llandaff 1971.
1972. Derrick Greenslade Childs. Consecrated 23 May 1972.
Also Archbishop of Wales. Enthroned Archbishop
15 March 1983.
Resigned as Archbishop and Bishop 30 June 1986.
1986. Royston Clifford Wright. Consecrated 18 October 1986.

(F) Swansea and Brecon

The Diocese of Swansea and Brecon (842,338 acres) covered
Breconshire, most of Radnorshire, and in Glamorgan the Gower
Peninsula and the neck of land joining it to Breconshire; since local
government reorganization in April 1974 it has included about two
thirds of Powys, half of West Glamorgan, and portions of Gwent
and Mid Glamorgan. It is the only Diocese to have a common
boundary with every other diocese in Wales. The total population
in 1981 was about 320,000; Easter Communicants in 1988 were
13,459.

It is divided into two Archdeaconries. The Archdeaconry of
Brecon includes the Rural Deaneries of Brecon (i), Brecon (ii),
Builth-Elwell, Crickhowell, Hay, and Maelienydd, and the
Archdeaconry of Gower includes the Rural Deaneries of Clyne,
Cwmtawe, Llwchwr, Penderi, Swansea, and West Gower.

This is the youngest Diocese in the Church in Wales. It was
formed out of the Diocese of St. Davids on 23 June 1923. The first
Bishop was the Right Reverend Edward Latham Bevan, formerly
Vicar and Archdeacon of Brecon and Bishop Suffragan of
Swansea. The Cathedral of St. John the Evangelist in Brecon, a
medieval priory church, is situated in delightful surroundings and
provides a dignified setting for great services.

The shape of the Diocese on the map is one of the most unusual
in the Anglican Communion. It stretches from Bugeildy to Rhosili
and includes two very contrasting areas. In the north the
Archdeaconry of Brecon is made up of most of the old counties of
Breconshire and Radnorshire, the former with considerable good
farming land and the latter more bleak and largely dependent on
sheep farming. Parishes here are small in population but large in
area, and many are grouped in big units of four, five, or more

churches. The southern part of the Diocese is largely urban and industrial, although it also includes the Gower Peninsula. The City of Swansea has an impressive parish church, that of St. Mary, re-consecrated in 1959 after its destruction in the blitz of 1941. It has recently become a collegiate church, staffed by ten full-time or part-time chaplains, including a chaplain to the large University College. Since the Second World War many new churches have been built in the suburbs of Swansea, which also contains the Cathedral of the Roman Catholic Bishop of Menevia. There is little Welsh in the Diocese outside the Swansea Valley and the western part of Breconshire.

The Bishop lives at Brecon, which is central for all parts of the Diocese, but almost 40 miles from the City of Swansea, where most of the population lives. From time to time there has been discussion of the creation of a Diocese of Swansea, but the problem of providing episcopal oversight for the rural northern part of the Diocese must be solved before a seventh bishop's throne in Wales can be set up in St. Mary's.

Bishops of Swansea and Brecon

1923. Edward Latham Bevan.
Consecrated Suffragan Bishop of Swansea
29 September 1915
Translated to Swansea and Brecon 1923.
Died 2 February 1934.

1934. John Morgan. Consecrated 22 May 1934.
Translated to Llandaff 1939.

1939. Edward William Williamson.
Consecrated 30 November 1939.
Died 23 September 1953.

1954. William Glyn Hughes Simon.
Consecrated 6 January 1954.
Translated to Llandaff 1957.

1958. John James Absalom Thomas.
Consecrated 25 January 1958.
Resigned 15 February 1976.

1976. Benjamin Noel Young Vaughan.
Consecrated Bishop Suffragan of Mandeville,
Jamaica, 29 June 1961.
Bishop of Swansea and Brecon 1976.
Resigned 25 December 1987.

1988. Dewi Morris Bridges. Consecrated 25 March 1988.

Appendix IV

A Hymn by Bishop Timothy Rees

This hymn, written by one of the greatest Bishops of the Church in Wales, expresses most poetically the hopes of Welsh Churchpeople for their Church. It is usually sung to the rousing tune Blaenwern.

'Lord, who in thy perfect wisdom
Times and seasons dost arrange—
Working out thy changeless purpose
In a world of ceaseless change:
Thou didst form our ancient nation
In remote barbaric days,
To unfold in it a purpose
To thy glory and thy praise.

To our shores, remote, benighted,
Washed by distant western waves,
Tidings in thy love thou sentest,
Tidings of the Cross that saves.
Men of courage strove and suffered
Here thy holy Church to plant:
Glorious in the roll of heroes
Shines the name of Dewi Sant.

Lord, we hold in veneration
All the saints our land has known,
Bishops, priests, confessors, martyrs
Standing now around thy throne—
Dewi, Dyfrig, Deiniol, Teilo,—
All the gallant saintly band,
Who of old by prayer and labour
Hallowed all our fatherland.

Still thy ancient purpose standeth
Every change and chance above;
Still thy ancient Church remaineth—
Witness to thy changeless love.
Vision grant us, Lord, and courage
To fulfil the work begun;
In the Church and in the nation
Lord of lords, thy will be done.'

Further Reading

A. Disestablishment

Bell, G. K. A.   *Randall Davidson, Archbishop of Canterbury* (1938)
Bell, P. M. H.   *Disestablishment in Ireland and Wales* (1969)
Cardiff Convention *Official Report of the Proceedings of the Convention of the Church in Wales...1917* (1917)
Davies, E. T.   *Disestablishment and Disendowment* (1970)
Ellis, T. I.   'Comisiwn yr Eglwys' in *John Humphreys Davies* (1963)
Jones, M.   'The Church in Wales after Disestablishment' in *The Church Quarterly Review* (1919)
Jones, R. T.   *Ffydd ac Argyfwng Cenedl, 1890-1914* (2 vols, 1981)
Morgan, K. O.   *Freedom or Sacrilege? A History of the Campaign for Welsh Disestablishment* (1966)
Tilney, C.   *The Church in Wales: The Disestablishment Conflict* (n.d.)
Walker, D.   'The Welsh Church and Disestablishment' in *The Modern Churchman (1971)*

B. General Works

Brierley, P. &
  Evans, B. (eds.)   *Prospects for Wales: Report of the 1982 Census of the Churches* (1983)
Church in Wales
  Board of Mission   *Faith in Wales* (1988)
Church in Wales   *Report of the Nation and Prayer Book Commission* (1949)
Church in Wales   *Handbook of the Welsh Church Congress, 1953* (1953)
Davies, E. T.   *Religion and the Industrial Revolution in South Wales* (1965)
Davies, E. T.   *A New Layman's Guide to the Church in Wales* (1967)

Davies, E. T.	*Religion and Society in Nineteenth-Century Wales* (1981)
Edwards, A.G.	*Landmarks in the History of the Church in Wales* (1913)
Ellis, T. I.	*Ym Mêr fy Esgyrn* (1955)
James, J. W.	*A Church History of Wales* (1945)
Keane, J. G. (ed.)	*Coming of Age* [Cymry'r Groes 1943-64] (1964)
Morgan, K. O.	*Wales in British Politics, 1868-1920* (1980 edition)
Morgan, K. O.	*Rebirth of a Nation: Wales 1880-1980* (1981)
Morgan, P. & Thomas, D. (eds.)	*Wales: The Shaping of a Nation* (1984)
Price, D. T. W.	'The Contribution of St. David's College, Lampeter, to the Church in Wales, 1920-1971' in the *The Journal of Welsh Ecclesiastical History* (1984)
Price, D. T. W.	'Church and Society in Wales since Disestablishment' in Badham, P.B.L. (ed.) *Religion, State, and Society in Modern Britain* (1989)
Price, D. T. W.	*A History of St. David's University College, Lampeter* (volume ii, 1898-1971) (1990)
Walker, D. (ed.)	*A History of the Church in Wales* (1976)
Williamson, E. W.	'The Church in Wales' in *Theology* (1948)
Williams, G.	*Religion, Language, and Nationality in Wales* (1979)

C. The Constitution of the Church in Wales

Church in Wales	*The Constitution of Church in Wales* (1988 edition)
Green, C. A. H.	*The Setting of the Constitution of the Church in Wales* (1937)

D. Dioceses and Local Areas

Davies, E. T. (ed.)	*The Story of the Church in Glamorgan 560-1960* (1962)
Diocese of Llandaff	*Report of the Llandaff Diocesan Commission* (1968)
Harris, C. C.	*Facing the Future Together: The Report of the Bangor Diocesan Survey* (1973)
Jones, O. W. & Walker, D. (eds.)	*Links with the Past: Swansea and Brecon Historical Essays* (1974)
Read, J. C.	*The Church in our City* [Cardiff] (1954)

Simon, G.	*A Time of Change* (1967)
Thomas, D. R.	*The History of the Diocese of St. Asaph* (1908-13)
Walker, D. and others	*Swansea and Brecon 1923-1973: The Jubilee of a Diocese* (1973)
Williams, G. O.	*The Church's Work* (1959)

E. The Archbishops and Bishops

Edwards, A. G.	*Memories* (1927)
Edwards, A. J.	'Bishop Green of Monmouth' in *The Journal of the Historical Society of the Church in Wales* (1971)
Edwards, A. J.	*Archbishop Green: His Life and Opinions* (1986)
Jones, O. W.	*Glyn Simon: His Life and Opinions* (1981)
Lerry, G.	*Alfred George Edwards, Archbishop of Wales* (1940)
Lerry, G.	'A. G. Cambrensis' in *The Journal of the Historical Society of the Church in Wales* (1947)
Lewis, E.	*John Bangor, the People's Bishop* (1962)
Owen, E. E.	*The Later Life of Bishop Owen* (1961)
Peat-Binns, J. S.	'Arglwydd Archesgob Cymru: Alfred Edwin Morris—Election and Afterwards' in *The Journal of Welsh Ecclesiastical History* (1985)
Peart-Binns, J. S.	*Archbishop Edwin Morris* (1990)
Rees, J. L.	*Timothy Rees of Llandaff and Mirfield* (1945)

F. Parish Life

Jones, D. P.	*A Welsh Country Parson* (1975)
Richards, D.	*Honest to Self* (1971)
Richards, D.	*Honest Memories* (1985)

G. Liturgy

Church in Wales	*Services and Ceremonies* [*Candlemas, Ash Wednesday, etc.*] (1983)
Church in Wales	*The Book of Common Prayer for Use in the Church in Wales* (vol. i) (1984)
Church in Wales	*The Book of Common Prayer for Use in the Church in Wales* (vol. ii) (1985)
Church in Wales	*The Holy Eucharist in Modern Language* (1984)

The Commission of the
  Covenanted Churches   *The Holy Communion* (1981)
Lewis, E.   *Prayer Book Revision in the Church in Wales*
                     (1958)

H. Reference Works

Church in Wales   *The Directory and Year Book of the Church in Wales* 1924, 1925.
Church in Wales   *The Welsh Church Year Book* 1929.
Church in Wales   *The Official Handbook of the Church in Wales* 1930, 1933, 1936, 1939, 1959.

I. Periodicals

Highlights
Impact
Province
The Welsh Churchman
Yr Haul
Y Llan